Poetry in Motion

Co Londonderry
Edited by Steve Twelvetree

Young Writers

First published in Great Britain in 2004 by:
Young Writers
Remus House
Coltsfoot Drive
Peterborough
PE2 9JX
Telephone: 01733 890066
Website: www.youngwriters.co.uk

All Rights Reserved

© Copyright Contributors 2004

SB ISBN 1 84460 387 3

Foreword

This year, the Young Writers' 'Poetry In Motion' competition proudly presents a showcase of the best poetic talent selected from over 40,000 up-and-coming writers nationwide.

Young Writers was established in 1991 to promote the reading and writing of poetry within schools and to the youth of today. Our books nurture and inspire confidence in the ability of young writers and provide a snapshot of poems written in schools and at home by budding poets of the future.

The thought effort, imagination and hard work put into each poem impressed us all and the task of selecting poems was a difficult but nevertheless enjoyable experience.

We hope you are as pleased as we are with the final selection and that you and your family continue to be entertained with *Poetry In Motion Co Londonderry* for many years to come.

Contents

Coleraine Academical Institution

Casey McKinney (13)	1
Matthew McKeown (14)	2
Gary Hutton (14)	3
Danail McArthur (13)	4
Andrew Ferris (12)	5
James Mills (13)	5
Gareth Steele (15)	6
Philip Taylor (14)	7
Robert Hart (13)	8
Matthew Adams (12)	9
Andrew Morrow (13)	10
Timothy Kelly (14)	10
Michael McDowell (12)	11
Peter Gilpin (14)	11
Jonathan Mitchell (12)	12
Aaron Evangelista (12)	12
Stephen Dobbin (14)	13
Dylan Frew (13)	13
Douglas Flatt (14)	14
Chris McAteer (15)	15
Alistair Adams (14)	16
Jesse Gordon (14)	16
Simon Caulfield (14)	17
Richard McCandless (12)	17
Jamie McBurney (13)	18
Maurice Tannahill (13)	18
Elliott Clarke (12)	19
John Martin (13)	19
Jody McGarvey (12)	20
Tom He (12)	21
Stuart Wilson (14)	22
Michael Topping (13)	23
Philip McAuley (13)	24
Karl Allen (12)	25
Ryan Gilmore (14)	26
Keith Taylor (13)	27
David Mawhinney (14)	28
Niall McDonagh (13)	29

Alan Gourley (14) — 30
David Lennox (14) — 31

Coleraine High School
Melonia Hamilton (14) — 32
Laura King (13) — 33
Lauren Skelton (14) — 34
Kylie McVicker (15) — 34
Amy Rowntree (14) — 35
Trudy Aiken (15) — 35
Muriel Bisby (14) — 36
Keri McFarlane (15) — 36
Leah Stewart (15) — 37
Elizabeth Crowe (15) — 37
Hannah Farthing & Louise Rowan (14) — 38
Rachel Gregg (14) — 38
Hannah Stevens (14) — 39
Natalie Donaghy (14) — 39
Stephanie Adair (14) — 40
Hollie Connolly (14) — 40
Mallorie Coyles (14) — 41
Janet Warke (14) — 41
Nicola Platt (14) — 42
Cheryl Mairs (14) — 42
Jenna Watt (13) — 43
Kirsty Speers (14) — 43
Hannah Harkness (14) — 44
Laura McKinney (14) — 44
Lauren Norris (14) — 45
Lisa McNabb (13) — 45
Tracy Carson (14) — 46
Catherine Morrison (14) — 46
Nicola Stirling (13) — 47
Helen Caldwell (14) — 47
Naomi Rea (13) — 48
Heather Ralph (14) — 48
Annie Hegarty (13) — 49
Linzi-Jane Black (13) — 49
Esther Alleyne (13) — 50
Abby McCracken (13) — 50
Kirsty Steele (13) — 51

Catherine Lamont (13)	51
Helen Aiken (13)	52
Hannah Hough (13)	52
Deborah Morrell (13)	53
Lauren Pratt (13)	53
Sarah Acheson (13)	54
Hayley Mearns (13)	55
Rachael Thompson (13)	56
Catherine Martin (13)	56
Nicola Claire Bacon (13)	57
Tara McLaughlin (13)	57
Catherine Paul (13)	58
Cate Cameron-Mitchell (11)	58
Julie Stockton (13)	59
Joy Cochrane (11)	59
Rebekah Robinson (13)	60
Victoria McQuilkin (13)	60
Katie Leighton (13)	61
Catherine Clarke (13)	62
Amy McPeak (13)	62
Charis Wray (11)	63
Jade Warwick (13)	63
Hilary Cameron (13)	64
Olivia Smith (13)	64
Emma Bannister (12)	65
Yasmin Flatt (12)	65
Leona Blair (12)	66
Shauna Bratten (12)	67
Cathy Callaghan (12)	68
Jenna Purcell (13)	68
Stephanie Craig (12)	69
Chlöe Dougan (12)	69
Olivia Esler (12)	70
Sarah Boyd (13)	70
Cherie Gamble (12)	71
Laura McFarlane (12)	71
Julianne Hegarty (12)	72
Rachel Black (11)	72
Ilea Hendron (12)	73
Sara Wilson (11)	73
Lauren Hunter (12)	74
Sarah Breen (11)	74

Emerald Owens (12)	75
Laura Kemps (11)	75
Suzanne Patton (12)	76
Claire Wilson (12)	76
Cathy McAlonan (13)	77
Shauna Platt (11)	77
Catherine Stewart (11)	78
Rachael McKeeman (13)	79
Lauren McCollum (11)	80
Naomi Dorrans (12)	80
Clare Taylor (11)	81
Tamsin McKissick (12)	81
Rui Wang (11)	82
Beth Eustace (12)	82
Sarah Robinson (11)	83
Rachel McGowan (12)	83
Lori Shirlow (11)	84
Diane Clyde (11)	84
Niamh Owens (11)	85
Vivien Lyons (11)	85
Lisa Douglas (11)	86
Rebecca Holley (11)	86
Catherine Tweed (11)	87
Louise Kane (11)	88
Chantelle Murdoch (11)	88
Zara Leighton (11)	89
Zoë Browne (11)	89
Kelly McAfee (11)	90
Emma McCrea (11)	90
Samantha Mairs (11)	91
Sarah Kirkpatrick (12)	91
Sirri Topping (11)	92
Rachel Smyth (11)	93
Jenna Scobie (11)	94
Natasha Spence (11)	94
Hazel Ramsey (11)	95
Nicola Andrews (12)	95
Claire McLaughlin (11)	96
Jenna McFaull (12)	96
Rebecca Henderson (13)	97
Robyn Jessica Millar (11)	97
Jennifer Crossley (12)	98

Emma Wray (12)	98
Gillian Wisener (12)	99
Lynsey Barr (12)	99
Helen Dobbin (12)	100
Sarah Minihan (13)	100
Carrie-Lyn Kane (12)	101
Emma Neill (13)	101
Gillian Simpson (12)	102
Claire Carson (12)	103
Aimée Hamilton (12)	104
Erin McCollum (12)	104
Emma Doherty (12)	105
Lauren Young (12)	105
Clare Reynolds (12)	106
Lauren Kettyle (12)	106
Hannah Kelly (13)	107
Amber Stewart (12)	107
Charlotte Kilgore (12)	108
Laura Doherty (12)	108
Gemma Webster (12)	109
Rebecca Dysart (12)	109
Julie Magee (13)	110
Elaine Hunter (13)	111
Jade McCook (13)	112
Zara McIntyre (13)	112
Heather Porter (12)	113
Stephanie Speers (12)	113
Kathryn Dobbin (12)	114
Emma Robson (12)	115
Holly McCullough (13)	116
Naomi Parkhill (13)	117
Jill Oliver (12)	117
Kerry Kilgore (12)	118

Kilronan Special School

Vincent McErlean (16)	118
Lisa Stockman (11)	119

Magherafelt High School

William Overend (13)	119
Stewart Miller (14)	120

Laura McKeown (13)	121
Neil Burns (13)	122
Lynsey Brown (13)	123
Victoria Cross (13)	124
Lauren Lennox (14)	125
Arran Fleming (13)	126
Rebecca Scott (13)	126
Danielle McIlhatton (13)	127
John Spallen (12)	127
Jennifer Brown (13)	128
Craig Ritchie (13)	129
Matthew Hagan (13)	130
Adam McMenemy (12)	130
Cordelia Mulholland (13)	131
Nevin Riddell (12)	131
Laura Henry (13)	132
Johanna Crawford (12)	133
Russell Fullerton (12)	134
Rachel Anderson (12)	134
Jonathan Houston (12)	135
Richard Hamilton (12)	135
Daniel Kelso (11)	136
Aaron Campbell (12)	136
Jaime Morrow (12)	137
Rebecca Sloan (12)	137
Ryan Love (12)	138
Jonathan Hurl (11)	138
Vicki McAllen (12)	139
Claire Craig (12)	139
Mark McClenaghan (12)	140
Melvin Fulton (12)	140
Catherine Dempsey (11)	141
Alyson Speer (11)	141
Vanessa Hawthorne (11)	142
Megan McKee (11)	142
Richard Brown (12)	143
Keipher Booth (11)	143
Andrew Simpson (11)	144
Catherine Young (11)	144
Elaine Wilson (11)	145
Bryan Nelson (11)	145
Kyle Austin (11)	146

Samantha Hagan (11)	146
Nathan Morrow (11)	147
Glenn Henry (11)	147
Jamie-Lee Harris (11)	148
Annie Stewart (11)	148
Gillian Brooks (11)	149
Ian Montgomery (13)	149
Katrina Steele (12)	150
Laura Davidson (12)	150
Stephanie Sloss (12)	151
Jermaine Elder (13)	151
Michaela Smyth (13)	152
James Johnston (13)	152
Anna Shiels (13)	153
Emma Hogg (13)	153
Dawn McMullan (12)	154
Ross Nicholl (12)	155
Nigel Speer (13)	156
Jill Henderson (12)	156
Christine Hurl (12)	157
Craig Moore (13)	157
Rachel Taylor (12)	158
Andrew Henry (13)	158
Nadine Redpath (12)	159
Andrew McClelland (13)	159
Philip Dickson (13)	160
Graham Kirkpatrick (12)	161
Chloe Anderson (12)	162
Jason Scott (12)	162
Ruth Scott (13)	163
David Allen (12)	163
Laura Gilmour (12)	164
Carly Murphy (13)	164
Kerry Halsall (13)	165
Claire Evans (13)	165
Olive Houston (14)	166
Adam Johnston (12)	166
Trevor Bates (13)	167
Lee Rutherford (13)	167
Henry Stewart (12)	168
Harry Evans (13)	168
Rachel Hilman (13)	169

Annette Henderson (13)	169
Brian Forsythe (12)	170
William Pickering (14)	170
Helen Hawthorne (11)	171
Lee Weir (13)	171
Matthew Stewart (11)	172
Paul Tang (13)	172
William McIlhatton (12)	173
Richard Patterson (11)	173
Richard Love (13)	174
Mervyn Bowman (11)	174
William McClenaghan (11)	175
Alan Hyndman (11)	175
Jan Arrell (11)	176
Gavin Brown (12)	176
Cherith Scott (14)	177
Julie Morton (11)	177
Lesley Jackson (13)	178
Melissa Irvine (11)	178
Matthew Gallick (13)	179
Aaron Ferguson (11)	180
David Barfoot (14)	181
Paul Johnston (13)	182
Alan Simpson (12)	183
Emma Campbell (14)	184
Karen Evans (13)	185
Pamela Stewart (14)	186
Kenny Bradley (13)	186
Andrea Watters (14)	187
Adam Kells (11)	187
Natasha Hillyard (11)	188
Mark McClelland (11)	189
Alanna Johnston (12)	190
Rachel Henry (12)	191
David McAllen (12)	192
Laura Anderson (11)	193
Steven Higgins (12)	194
Alixs Ferguson (12)	194
Aaron McLean (11)	195
Lauren Scott (11)	196
Samantha Speirs (11)	197
Diane Booth (11)	198

David Burrows (12)	199
Nicky Brown (11)	200
David Mawhinney (11)	201
Leigh Gibson (11)	202

North Coast Integrated College

Robin O'Neill (11)	202
Jaimie White (17)	203
Linda Stewart (11)	203
Alistair Alan Chambers (12)	204
Justin Kane (11)	205
Reuben Hasson (11)	206
Paul McAlister (11)	206
Charlotte Beckett (12)	207
Natasha McCloskey (11)	207
Anna Reid (11)	208
Lauren Millar (11)	208
Matthew George Caulfield (11)	209
Stacey Kirgan (11)	210
Nicole McElwee (11)	211
Michael McConnell (17)	212
Stuart Kane (11)	212

Rainey Endowed School

Christine Gogarty (13)	213
Gemma Donnelly (17)	214

St Mary's Grammar School, Magherafelt

Vincent McKenna (11)	215
Katie McGuckian (13)	216
Johanna McAuley (12)	217
Michael Mullan (12)	218

Thornhill College

Damhnáit Mc Hugh (13)	218
Deborah Boyle (14)	219
Éimear Barr (13)	219
Stacey Concannon (13)	220
Hannah Mahon (12)	220
Eimear Doherty (11)	221

Nikita McChrystal (13)	221
Rachael Page (13)	222
Anna McKinney (14)	223
Clódagh McBay (12)	223
Gemma Houston (11)	224
Róisín Lautman (13)	224
Laura Doherty (11)	225
Lauren McDaid (13)	225
Claire Cassidy (12)	226
Natasha Deeney (13)	226
Sophie Dechant (13)	227
Rebecca Harkin	227
Milissa Deane (13)	228
Áine Laughlin (11)	228
Dearbhla McEleney (11)	229
Cara Duddy (12)	229
Una Kelly (12)	230
Seanna Meehan (11)	230
Aoife McTernan (12)	231
Clare McLaughlin (13)	231
Sarah Wallace (12)	232
Martina Murray (13)	232
Eimear McIvor (11)	233
Sharon Duffy (11)	233
Orla Hegarty (11)	234

The Poems

The Annual Tidy Up

There comes a day in every year,
Just one day, the day I fear,
I prepare the net, the gloves and broom,
It's now or never, time to tidy my room!

I step through the door
And stare at the mess,
Clothes on the floor,
Socks, shirts and vests,
Bowls full of cornflakes,
Growing with fur,
Old squashed cupcakes,
Some tackle and allure,
It's heaving with termites
And I'm covered in flea bites!
But it's been this way for thirteen years,
It's now my duty to face my fears.

So with my dog by my side
And a bag within reach,
I'll swallow my pride
And I can only preach,
That I can round up the mice,
Scrape up the rice,
Dig out the junk,
Get rid of the skunk
And separate all the clothes,
All while holding my nose.

Seven hours after,
I step out the door
And I think with laughter,
I'm safe for one year more!

Casey McKinney (13)
Coleraine Academical Institution

Hell's Angel

You have betrayed me
Now you shall pay for sin
No longer a soldier of Heaven
But the scum of Hell.

Words that were spoken
Millions of years ago
To an angel
Banished from Heaven to Hell.

His wings scorched black
By the fires of sin
He fell into these fires
And burst out reborn
Like a phoenix from the ashes.

He planned his revenge
An attack on Heaven
To destroy the one who took his wings.

Hell came erupting from the earth
Heaven from the skies
The darkness could not overcome the light
Hell could not help but die.

These powers will erupt again some day
No one knows when
But when they do
It shall be Earth that pays.

Matthew McKeown (14)
Coleraine Academical Institution

Seasons Of The Year

The days are getting colder,
The autumn wind is bolder,
Away go the colourful leaves,
We're left with the naked trees.

Christmas snow is falling,
Winter has come calling,
It's like a long, cold, frosty night,
Will we ever see the light?

Is that a snowdrop I can see
Underneath that apple tree?
Spring is on its way at last,
Winter soon is in the past.

In the fields the new lambs play,
'Spring is here,' they seem to say,
In the garden daffodils sway,
Warm summer is on its way.

The temperature begins to rise,
A day to the beach is no surprise,
Enjoy these days while they last,
For all too soon they will have passed.

Seasons come and seasons go,
Each has its own high and low,
Summer, autumn, winter, spring,
Each one different things they bring.

Gary Hutton (14)
Coleraine Academical Institution

The Seasons

I like spring - new life - I'm glad,
But I hate all those wasps,
They make me mad.
I'm lucky because I've never been stung,
My mum has once,
Right on her thumb!

Summer is good too,
The end of term,
Another year through,
Two whole months without school,
Let the fun begin!
Summer's cool!

Autumn, a brilliant time,
Collecting conkers,
Can yours beat mine?
Different leaves, green, yellow, red,
It's getting dark early
Time for bed.

Winter, definitely the best,
My favourite season,
It outranks the rest,
Look! Snow's finally falling,
Super! Brilliant!
Time for snowballing!

Danail McArthur (13)
Coleraine Academical Institution

Silence Is Golden

'Masks on!'
A frenzy of excitement is triggered
A sea of tumbling as gas masks are pulled on in a moment of panic.

A river of green gas flows in our direction
Silence, an eerie silence
Only disturbed by the faint trembling of fingers on triggers.

Streams of civilians are running, running,
Running to the bomb shelter. Dropping dead like stones into a river
Bodies fast carpeting the cobbled streets.

Screams of pain and despair pollute the air
You could stop these screams
Say no to war
Silence is golden.

Andrew Ferris (12)
Coleraine Academical Institution

Bloody Sunday - A March For Rights

A march for freedom,
A march for rights.
A march that would not last the night.
With the deadly paras out of sight,
A march that would turn into a fight.

The bullets flew,
The bodies fell.
Somehow reminiscent of Hell.
They would not stop,
They would not cease,
Till everyone was at *peace*.

Yet years have passed
And very fast . . .
The trial still goes on.
There is no cease, there is no peace.
How long will it last?

James Mills (13)
Coleraine Academical Institution

The Piper's Poem

The bag lies empty
And the chanter silent,
As when young Jonny lifts to play,
What a present he's received on this very special day.

No note is visible,
Between the long, low-pitched drone,
Young Jonny needs coaching,
'Else his pipes lie useless.

Gracefully his father takes the pipes
And begins a hearty tune
And as his father before him,
He teaches Jonny this skilful craft.

Jonny learns as his father teaches,
For young Jonny knows he must succeed,
Just like his father before him,
Jonny must become the best.

Jonny has learnt his skilful craft
And become the best of them all.
Now Jonny must pass his skill and wisdom,
To his own bonny son.

Now young Jonny is old and gone,
Now again his bag lies empty
And his chanter silent
And the drones of his pipes are heard no more.

Gareth Steele (15)
Coleraine Academical Institution

The Boy Done Well

It was a long time ago,
Many years of working hell,
Before his father could say,
'My boy done well!'

He started at the bottom,
Could only dream of playing at the top.
Never shone at under thirteens,
Many thought he didn't have a shot.

Never understood the point of school,
Spent all his time kicking ball at wall.
His homework was always late or badly done.
He thought of nothing else but football.

Played with the youths until he was old enough,
Worked out and got fit, until he was good enough.
He featured big in the training at Bellefield,
Then broke to the fringes for the team at Goodison.

Battled his way into the Blues' first team side,
Worked hard in midfield week in, week out.
He had his critics, who disliked his style
And some of the fans began to doubt.

His first goal came at Goodison today.
He set up two more for others to score
And now the papers are singing his praises,
In cries of adulation: 'That boy done well!'

Philip Taylor (14)
Coleraine Academical Institution

When The Going Gets Tough, The Tough Get Rowing

Just off, get ready to row.
The sun is shining so, 'Boys, let's roll.'
Splishing and splashing to the beat,
Don't have time to look at your feet.

The river's long,
The oars heavy.
The going's good
We're more than ready.

Time's passing, feeling sore,
Heads spinning, more and more.
Sweat dripping off us, now and again.
Need a drink. 'Not till the end!'

Our hearts beating;
Hands pumping
We're near the finish line,
So get in line.

'Ten firm! Next stroke! . . . Go!'

The cox screams at us
We feel the adrenaline
So tired we can barely breathe.
Panting and shouting, we give it our best!

Tired as can be!
We must try, we must try!
So row your hardest
We'll get by, we'll get by.

Crossed the finish line - so pleased!
'Wind down,' says the cox
Our muscles feel like jelly,
But hey - we did it, we did it!

Robert Hart (13)
Coleraine Academical Institution

Adrenaline Rush

The engines roar
The bikes soar
I'm flying like a swallow.

We're on the straight
I up the rate
The other racers follow.

I really need
To take the lead
I could be number one.

I'm racing third
Swift as a bird
I'm really having fun.

The adrenaline rush
The crowds all hush
I'm passing number two.

I pick up speed
And take the lead
I come out of the blue . . .

The last bend!
It is the end!
I've beaten all the rest!

I'm really proud
I shout out loud
'I've won this year's North West!'

Matthew Adams (12)
Coleraine Academical Institution

The Somme

When the word came,
They thought it was sane,
So they went over the top,
And the enemy guns started to pop.

But they had little chance,
That fateful day in France,
For the order was not wise,
But an order for their demise.

One million men in all,
And Germany still did not fall,
Six miles they did gain,
All their lives were lost in vain.

But the generals safe in their den,
Did not see the soldiers as men,
But pawns in their games,
Soulless fighters with no names.

Andrew Morrow (13)
Coleraine Academical Institution

The Wind

Moving silently from place to place,
But no one knows where,
It passes like snow on the mountains,
It is wind in the meadow.

Its hostility increases,
Furiously it wanders the barren lands,
All that has been left is wreckage,
All havoc has ceased.

Sleeping like a dragon
He holds his peace,
The stillness has been restored,
But it will not be prolonged.

Timothy Kelly (14)
Coleraine Academical Institution

The English Homework

The English teacher said, 'Write a poem
And have it in on time!
If you want to be really clever,
You can even make it rhyme!'

I sat for hours and hours on end,
Wondering what to say.
I could write about my family and friends
And what they did each day.

But no matter how much I tried to think,
Of something original to write.
The blank page on my computer screen,
Only exasperated my plight!

It's nine-thirty in the evening,
My imagination is starting to wear.
I looked at my computer screen,
And a poem was already there!

Michael McDowell (12)
Coleraine Academical Institution

McDonald's

McDonald's is a favourite of girls and boys,
To appeal to the kids they give free toys,
Anyone with common sense,
Would hold on to their ninety-nine pence.

The price of beef is more than that,
So they must serve you guts and fat.
The chips they make are short and thin,
Chicken nuggets are beaks and skin.

But after enjoying a 'Happy Meal'
A tempting dessert has much appeal,
So if you're not in much of a hurry,
Relax and enjoy a synthetic McFlurry!

Peter Gilpin (14)
Coleraine Academical Institution

The Thief In The Night

The thief in the night just creeps by,
Nobody knows that he's there.
As silent as shadows,
Swift as a hawk -
Not even the mice are aware.

As poor as a penny,
Gentle as a dove,
He wouldn't hurt a flea on a dog's bare back.
Surprising then he's not more desired,
A mysterious one so unloved.

The thief in the night just creeps by,
He searches your house till dawn's light.
Taking only as needed,
And leaving the rest,
He's away like an owl in flight!

Jonathan Mitchell (12)
Coleraine Academical Institution

A Bully/My Friend

There is a boy who lives near me
Who thinks he's really hard,
As far as I can see,
He's a bully and a coward.

One day he tried to pick a fight,
So I arranged to meet him that night.

Out we came with our fists flinging,
I left him on the ground with his ears ringing.

So those of you who pick on others,
Will be sent home crying to your mothers.

From that night I've had no bother,
In fact, we're best friends with each other.

Aaron Evangelista (12)
Coleraine Academical Institution

Where Your Dreams Go

Did you ever wonder where your dreams go?
When the world gets in your way,
When you're told you're not good enough,
And you don't know what to say.

Did you ever want to be a teacher?
Or even a headmaster?
But then you went and messed it up,
And now your life's a disaster.

Did you ever wonder what's wrong with the world?
And why no one cares,
Wars are fought every day,
Are you the only one it scares?

Did you ever wonder where your dreams go?
When the world gets in your way,
But what's the point in screaming?
When no one's listening anyway.

Stephen Dobbin (14)
Coleraine Academical Institution

What They Don't Know

What they don't know
They will make up
Add bits on and make life rough
They don't care how it makes you feel
The hurt they cause is never enough.
Day by day, things don't improve.
What they don't know is they are the fools
They just show off for all their worth
They ridicule and tease and push and shove
When in their gang they think they can't lose
What they don't know is they've already lost
They may be feared but they're not respected
For making others feel dejected.

Dylan Frew (13)
Coleraine Academical Institution

My Grandpa

My grandpa's name is Jack,
Very special to me,
A man for whom I really care,
He fills my face with glee.

He used to live in Scotland,
Kirkcaldy to be precise,
He lived there with his wife,
They were a couple with no strife.

While I sat beside him,
I remember all the fun we had,
Talking together happily,
It made me very glad.

When he came to visit me,
He filled my face with happiness,
I wish he could be with me now,
But he's in a better place.

He was very, very old,
Ninety-five to be exact,
He didn't have much hair,
But I never really used to care.

He never ever had a doubt,
With God and his wife at his side,
I love him just as much,
Just, as if he were alive.

Douglas Flatt (14)
Coleraine Academical Institution

Teenage Hair Advisors On The Dole

Democracy made a faux pas
So the scapegoats are on a hey day
Scared?
Then hide behind your cannon fodder
We're the tasty morsels
Eat up, then get more souls
Get yourself armed
And enforce some fear
Teenage hair advisors
Are on the dole
God's in colour
But that's not what they're watching TV for
Demons hide the bogeymen
So the politicians can infect our children's minds
Pass the parcel
With bigot propaganda inside
AIDs on the rise
So be careful when shaking hands
Private cocktails intoxicate the rich
While the homeless are shot at from hotel windows
Beware while crossing
Hollywood cowboys may trample you down.

Chris McAteer (15)
Coleraine Academical Institution

Struggle

Booms crashing,
Sails flailing,
Rigging creaking,
Struggling to keep in control,
Lost in the vast ocean of loneliness,
No land in sight,
No visible support,
No way of knowing where to go,
Struggling amongst waves of disappointment,
Lost, helpless,
In waters unknown,
Going in circles,
Losing hope, nearly giving up,
Light breaks through,
Rays of hope tearing through the once choking clouds,
Worn and ragged sails, filled with new strength,
Land looming before the once lost craft,
The journey is over,
Torn and dented,
A small vessel proudly returns home.

Alistair Adams (14)
Coleraine Academical Institution

Skateboarding

S is for the streets where skaters skate about
K is for kickflip a class flip trick
A is for axle grind when you grind on one track
T is for Tony Hawk, one of the greatest skaters in the world
E is for extreme which is what skating is all about
B is for backflip, a really hard trick
O is for ollie, the first basic trick
A is for astonishing, that's what skaters are
R is for reckless, which some of them can be
D is for darkslide, the coolest grind of all.

Jesse Gordon (14)
Coleraine Academical Institution

Depression

Depression can be seen far and wide,
From a place of money, to a place of pride,
Children are crying, tears running down their cheek,
No food, no family, the future seems bleak,
Fighting is happening nearly all the time,
Loved one's dying, no thought of a crime.

Delight can be seen in a place of pleasure,
But some don't have memories, or thoughts to treasure,
Rich people are likely to be found in a home,
Yet some of our neighbours are living on their own,
With nothing to keep which will come to please,
Maybe only the chance of catching disease.

Joy can be seen without a relationship of love,
Many can only dream the sight of a dove,
Feeling distressed about the ache of their heart,
No water anywhere is always the worst
There's no one to pick them up when they fall,
It seems this depression will never become small.

Simon Caulfield (14)
Coleraine Academical Institution

Grand Prix

Michael Schumacher's Ferrari is seventh on the grid
It turns the first corner fast into a skid
He passes each car picking up speed
In a matter of time he regains the lead.

He pulls into the pits and gets new tyres put on
The car's fuelled up and in ten seconds he's gone
He's on the last lap and still in first place
He takes the chequered flag to win the race.

Richard McCandless (12)
Coleraine Academical Institution

Teachers

Are all teachers human
Or do they come from Mars?
Do they eat and sleep
Or drive supersonic cars?

What is in the staffroom?
A golf course, a market, some chairs?
Somewhere to relax,
Or place some gambling dares?

Are they all vampires,
Headmaster being the boss?
Or are they all werewolves,
Whose path you wouldn't cross?

But as long as I know one thing,
That'll be OK,
Teachers are obviously human
Aren't they . . .

Jamie McBurney (13)
Coleraine Academical Institution

The Dog

There's an old, grey dog that lives in the park
And if you go near it, it really can bark!
It growls and growls and shows its teeth,
But why it's there, is beyond belief!

It must be a stray,
I thought one day!
The owner must have chucked it out,
Another unwanted, no doubt!

I asked my dad if I could have it,
He said, 'No, it would only cause havoc!'
I really wanted the poor, old thing,
But my daddy told me to 'Go and sing!'

Maurice Tannahill (13)
Coleraine Academical Institution

Young Writers - Poetry In Motion Co Londonderry

Tara

This loveable hound
From Norway came,
She left the sleighs
For our little lane.

After school every day
Without fail,
She runs up to meet me
With her wagging tail.

Running around
Without any care
Acting an edjit
Leaving hairs everywhere.

Tara's big and lazy
But she's my fluffy friend
And may the hours of fun she brings me
Never, ever end.

Elliott Clarke (12)
Coleraine Academical Institution

Home

Home is where I trust anyone,
Home is where my mum serves lunch,
Home is where I play the PC,
Home is where I love to be.

Home is where work's never done,
Home is good when you're having fun,
Home is where I'm always welcome,
Home is like my private world.

Home is like a prince's palace,
Home is where I sleep at night,
There really is no place like home
Home is where I wrote this poem.

John Martin (13)
Coleraine Academical Institution

Poverty's Child

Poverty's child, skin pale white,
Battles for life, he's in the fight.

'I battled hard, it was tough,
But it looks like I didn't battle hard enough.

I'm up above now, I'm with the Lord,
I'm in my own special ward.

On the door I did read,
Poverty's child, child in need.

I stopped to think what I did on Earth,
I did nothing, I was a waste of a birth,
I was just a mistake,
What kind of man would I ever make?

But as I said, I'm up above
And I am something, something to love,
Up there, I've got a friend,
He is great, His love won't end.

I'm better up here,
Help - it is near
And not in me is an ounce of fear.

Time to go, got to live,
I have ten years of love to give.'

Jody McGarvey (12)
Coleraine Academical Institution

School

At 7am it's time to get up
And the sun shines its rays,
At 8.45 warning bells ring,
Students whine, ready for
Another school day,
About the science, question six,
Or wasn't the technology about the structure of bricks?

At 9.05 off to class we go,
Are the lessons full of action? Usually no,
10.55, break time at last,
Thought the morning would never go past.

12.45, lunchtime - the best,
Just wish the work wasn't such a pest,
After food, football on the field,
Hope the good weather doesn't fail.

3.25, home time again,
There might be a day without homework
But the question is when?
What's the point of boring homework most nights,
I'll protest against homework when the time is right!

Tom He (12)
Coleraine Academical Institution

War

All these world leaders just make me sick,
Bush, Hussein or Blair, take your pick,
All these adults arguing all the time,
Over what? Cowardly bombs hidden in a mine.

Heads of state seem to be hell-bent,
On sending peacekeepers, they came and went,
Negotiations fail time and time again,
With the loss of life, women and men.

Terrorists are cowards, they can't agree, they have to kill,
Their only rule is to fire at will,
Shooting people because of their race,
Also their culture and the colour of their face.

Agreement. All we have to do is communicate,
Those leaders might even save their states,
Being open isn't as bad as we think,
It helps keep countries back from the brink.

Stuart Wilson (14)
Coleraine Academical Institution

Autumn

The school days have started
The birds have gone away,
The days are shorter
And farmers bring in their hay.

The autumn leaves are falling,
Red, yellow and brown,
The wind is stronger
And the rain comes tumbling down.

All the happy tourists,
Pack their bags and go,
The beaches are now empty
As the tide ebbs to and fro.

Animals collect their food,
For winter is growing near,
No more games of football,
Because autumn is now here.

Michael Topping (13)
Coleraine Academical Institution

InstitutionThe Flight

My hands were sweaty as I boarded the plane,
To you this probably sounds insane.
My dad told me that we would be safe,
I crossed my fingers just in case.

I was nervous and anxious and I needed to eat,
As we waited around to be shown our seat.
I was stuck to my seat as we hurtled down the strip,
And I closed my eyes trying not to flip.

In the air wasn't too bad,
I watched a movie with my dad.
I'd still be glad to get back on the ground,
Back to earth, safe and sound.

As we started to descend my hands got wet,
We were still ten minutes away yet.
Everyone could see the runway in sight,
Although it was dark, coming into the night.

As we were coming into land,
My mouth felt like it was filling up with sand.
We got back onto the ground,
I was back safe and sound.

Philip McAuley (13)
Coleraine Academical Institution

Race Day

Waiting at the starting line
I don't feel very fine.
My knees are shaking
And my head is aching.

The bikes are roaring
In a minute we are soaring.
I am flying down the track
With boys at my back.

The steep hills
Give me a thrill.
The mud is churned
As we twist and turn.

Once I see that finish line
I want this race to be mine.
I am head to head to win the race
I must not lose, this is my chase!

As I open the throttle
I think, *Karl don't lose your bottle!*
The glory is mine
I will never forget this time
As I cross the finish line.

Karl Allen (12)
Coleraine Academical Institution

My Hero

I was never a believer,
In magical philosophy,
It all just seemed so bland,
Until he inspired me.

I'd watch him on the TV
And read about him too,
It never seemed possible,
What this man could do.

He'd perform amazing illusions
And put on a breathtaking show,
He would always strike a smile,
Wherever he would go.

But now he's in his box,
Forty-four days and nights,
Suspended over the River Thames,
Don't worry, he'll win the fight.

But for him it doesn't matter,
About the money or the fame,
For him it's about the magic,
My hero, David Blaine.

Ryan Gilmore (14)
Coleraine Academical Institution

The Match

Football, football,
The beautiful game,
Millions of supporters,
To win is their aim.

Kick-off, kick-off,
The match has begun,
30 minutes later,
We're winning 2-1.

Coming round the stadium
A Mexican wave,
Rooney with a volley,
But a very good save.

Penalty, penalty,
That's a foul!
You're losing 3-1,
So throw in the towel.

Full time, full time,
The match is won,
Everton win,
By 3 goals to 1.

Keith Taylor (13)
Coleraine Academical Institution

Poetry In Motion

The players run out, one by one,
All the hard work and training is finally done,
The opposing team on the pitch they meet,
Everyone watching is at the edge of their seat.

The whistle blows to start the match,
The first high ball goes to the goalie, what a catch!
There are a lot of chances and nerves run high,
But it's now half-time and it's still a tie.

After the break the players come back out,
'Let's get to it, boys!' the captain is heard to shout,
It's nearly full time when round the ankles, Mike's caught,
'Penalty,' exclaims the referee and points to the spot.

It's Mike who steps up to strike the ball,
A small reward for a nasty fall,
He places the ball in the bottom corner with ease
And then with relief, sinks to his knees.

The whistle blows and the best team has won,
The manager is congratulated, 'Very well done!'
The crowd jumps up to shout and clap,
As the team holds the trophy high on their victory lap.

David Mawhinney (14)
Coleraine Academical Institution

Write A Poem

Write a poem
On your favourite CD
Then you can play it
To your friends and me.

Write a poem
With chocolate sauce
Swirled in your ice cream
Oh, what a loss!

Write a poem
On your mobile phone
Then text your mum
When you're late home.

Write a poem
On your bedroom wall
If it gets too long
Go into the hall.

Write a poem
It's lots of fun
And you'll be pleased
With what you've done.

Niall McDonagh (13)
Coleraine Academical Institution

Formula One Racing

F errari start again on pole
O thers try to reach the goal
R unning engines one, two, three
M ichael Schumacher takes the lead
U gly start for Jaguars
L osing out to other cars
A nother car is falling back.

O il is spilt on the track
N ow the yellow flags are out
E verybody's losing out.

R alf has caught up on his brother
A nd Michael has to push it further
C oulthard takes out a Renault Elf
I n which Kimi has to do it himself
N ow they reach the final bend
G oing over the finish first, Michael's race is at an end.

Alan Gourley (14)
Coleraine Academical Institution

Life

Life is something wonderful
Full of happiness and bliss
It truly is amazing
How much someone can miss.

We never know what happens next
We only can expect
We also wish for something more
Rather than appreciate what we get.

Life's path can change in an instant
From happy to sad
But we should not despair
For people are always there to help us if we need it.

Life is something we should treasure
Something we should not measure
Sometimes it can cause a commotion
It truly is poetry in motion.

David Lennox (14)
Coleraine Academical Institution

Term Begins Again

I wake up early
in bed again
clock ringing loud
in my ear again

stand freezing
at the bus stop again
rubbing my hands
to get warm again

the teachers
dispirited and cross
again

the old grey lockers
which refuse to shut
again

the science nightmare
I don't understand
again

the bell rings loudly
attempting to deafen me
again

back at the bus stop
bored waiting
again

get home
tackle homework
again

I have nightmares of school
                            again
                            and again

I wake up early
in bed again

clock ringing loud
in my ear

again.

Melonia Hamilton (14)
Coleraine High School

Nuts About Chocolate

Chocolate, chocolate, everybody loves it
Smooth and creamy, why is it so bad?
From chocolate cake to chocolate chips
Without chocolate, life is so sad.

It rots your teeth and makes you fat
And you would not like to be like that!
You'll end up going to the gym
To keep your figure nice and slim.

At special times throughout the year
That's when you will start to fear
But if you do not have the will
Eating chocolate is such a thrill.

From chocolate eggs to chocolate mice
You can even buy a chocolate ice!
Why can't it be good for you
And do the things that fruit can do?

So Mr Cadbury, you won the race,
You made your chocolate, which is ace
From that tiny cocoa bean
If only *first* I'd had that dream.

I would not be at school today,
In fact I would be far away
With money made from chocolate bars
Perhaps I'd go and live on Mars.
(I mean the planet!)

Laura King (13)
Coleraine High School

Autumn

The farmers gather all their crops,
Now they have their winter stock.
The hibernating animals,
Tuck themselves away,
Waiting for a warmer day.
The autumn leaves begin to fall,
While sleeves of corn are standing tall.
Forest fruits grow in their droves,
While many a mother stands over her stove.
The longer nights are setting in,
As we sit close to our next of kin.
As with all the seasons,
People celebrate for different reasons,
As Hallowe'en draws ever near,
Pumpkins and sparklers begin to appear.
Little mice scamper across the fields,
Until they meet the combine harvester's wheels.
The hungry birds swoop into the trees,
Sheltering themselves from the autumn breeze.
Children dress up in their Hallowe'en costumes,
And they have 'trick or treat' for so long,
That they are filled with exhaustion,
And these are the signs that autumn is here.

Lauren Skelton (14)
Coleraine High School

Autumn

Twirling, burling and dancing around,
Leaves carpet the cold, damp ground,
No longer can green ones be found,
All that can be heard is a loud, crispy sound.

Wind gushes and makes itself heard,
To miss summer - you must be absurd,
Spring, summer, winter, fall,
I know which one I like best of all.

Kylie McVicker (15)
Coleraine High School

Term Begins Again

Here I am, Monday morning
Dreaming again
Longing for
Summer holidays again

Dragging myself
Out of bed again
Dreading the homework
And teachers again

Rusty old lockers
And padlocks again
Form meetings
And assembly again

Some fun
In the lunch room again
Then back
To classes once again

The end of school
Bell rings in our ears again
I think then
Only 4 days to the weekend again.

Amy Rowntree (14)
Coleraine High School

Winter's Gone, Spring Is Here

Winter's gone and spring is here at last,
The sun's come out and the lambs are learning fast,
The fresh new flowers springing up from the ground,
Bring splashes of colour all around.
The trees gain leaves, the grass grows green,
The sky turns blue, to add to this scene,
The children come out to laugh and play,
This year does begin in the most wonderful way.

Trudy Aiken (15)
Coleraine High School

Anger!

With fiery red eyes and a roasting red face,
his blood began to boil.
Niggling comments turned from annoyance
to outrage and his temper began to uncoil.

Bitter and resentful thoughts
grew and grew.
With clenched fists and gnarled teeth,
his temper began to show through.

Sickening, painful memories
flood his every thought.
Revenge and hatred,
a force that cannot be caught.

Let free to wreak havoc,
a force with no bounds.
Flying fist on attack,
landing with bone-breaking sounds.

Muriel Bisby (14)
Coleraine High School

The Coming Of Winter

The ground starts to turn white,
Footprints are left behind.
Everything is silent,
Whilst the robins flutter around.
The trees are brown and bare,
With long sprawled out arms.
Among the mist and frost,
The holly berries begin to appear.
Some animals disappear and sleep,
The rivers start to get cold and deep.

Keri McFarlane (15)
Coleraine High School

The Coming Of Christmas

Darkness falls so early,
Darkness fades so late,
The howling wind blows the opening and closing gate
Through the grey mist the moon and stars set
The white snow falls all night long, in the dark and wet.

Hanging baubles around the prickly tree
All different colours of blue, red and green
Sitting around a burning fire
Faces red-raw and tired
Pulling crackers and telling jokes.

Beyond the brown, bare trees and far away,
Hills are covered in snow, like a white bubbling froth,
Snow falls like a white blanket again
The ice rain falls hard with a pitter
The cold frost sets and shimmers like glitter.

Leah Stewart (15)
Coleraine High School

The Coming Of Christmas

Fairy lights brighten the room
Like fireworks going off in the night
Presents stacked as high as a castle
With the blazing fire reflecting the light.
Cheeky robin hopping and bouncing
As the snow comes drifting down
Little children crunching through the snow
With warm woolly hats and boots covering their toes.
All the family gathering together
With open arms, and hugs exchanged.
This is the time I love the best
With winter nights and Christmas tree rays.

Elizabeth Crowe (15)
Coleraine High School

A Sonnet On The Sea

Above the salty depths that rise and fall,
Rolling with the sea breeze from shore to shore,
Cormorants skim the surface as they call,
And above them the seagulls glide and soar.
With the start of each day, new waves unfold,
The vast, endless, deep ocean swells and shrinks.
The colours change from cool blue to warm gold,
As the quick setting sun behind it sinks.

Below the surface lies a different tale,
The creatures are stirring, something's not right.
The fish dart from the outline of a whale,
Their predator near, no escape in sight.
What is in the depths will never be shown,
But what is above will always be known.

Hannah Farthing & Louise Rowan (14)
Coleraine High School

Night Fishing On The Lake

The steady dip of wooden oars,
Shattering the eerie silence,
Ripples manipulating the surface,
Of the bottomless black lake.

Floating there in solitude,
Drifting through the dark,
A lonesome old fisherman,
Casts out his nets.

He waits patiently in the dark
Hoping for a decent catch
To feed his family
Before they starve.

Rachel Gregg (14)
Coleraine High School

The Cat

Feet padding softly on the floor,
Silently pushing open the door,
On the soft armchair it lies,
Keeping watch with observant eyes.

Stealthily creeping through the night,
Preying on mice to its delight,
Forever watching, forever listening,
Then excitedly pouncing, eyes glistening.

Craftily slipping inside in the morning,
Propping itself on the sofa and yawning,
Constantly spoiled with treats and cat food,
All transferring it into a purring, happy mood.

Lots of scratch marks left on the wall,
Unravelled string along the hall,
It has its fun, then sleeps like a log,
Until abruptly awakened by the dog.

Hannah Stevens (14)
Coleraine High School

Love, What It Means To Me!

As he walks into the room
I realise how much he means to me
his deep, soothing voice I could listen to all day
his soft, subtle eyes just take my breath away.
As I look at him closely, a smile comes upon my face
soon returned by his which makes my blood race.
His pure personality is truly one of a kind
I never stop thinking about him, he's always on my mind.
He never seems to reveal just what he feels for me
but I'm sure I've made my feelings clear
he means the world to me.

Natalie Donaghy (14)
Coleraine High School

Start Of Term . . . Again!

1st of September comes . . . again
Alarm clock rings and shakes . . . again
Put on our green uniform . . . again
It's the start of term . . . again

Get on the school bus . . . again
Reach the same old school . . . again
See all our old teachers . . . again
It's the start of term . . . again

Go to first assembly . . . again
Listen to Mrs Hutchinson . . . again
Going on at us . . . again
It's the start of term . . . again

Now we're back at school . . . again
All of our new classes . . . again
Go by same old rules . . . again
It's the start of term . . . *again!*

Stephanie Adair (14)
Coleraine High School

Term Begins Again!

I hear the alarm go off, again,
And Mum yelling, 'Get up!' again,
Putting on my green uniform, again,
Waiting for the bus, again.

Standing in assembly, again,
Listening to the announcements, again,
On my way to class, again,
What's next? Oh yes, maths, again.

Homework's piling up, again,
Assignments due, again,
I wish the bell would ring, again,
So I could go home, again.

Hollie Connolly (14)
Coleraine High School

Apples

The forbidden fruit
Of the garden of Eden
It looks so tempting
Its bright green skin

It feels of leather
It smells so sweet
The shape is bulging
Like an unborn child
From the outside world

You taste the sweetness
As the juices ooze out
It's trickling down your chin
When you take a bite

Eat it quick
Before it turns brown

Your treat will be spoilt
If you try and savour the time.

Mallorie Coyles (14)
Coleraine High School

The Coming Of Winter

As I look out of the window I see,
Snowflakes falling from the sky, like leaves falling off the trees.
Robins cowering in the corner, trying to get out of the cold,
Icicles hanging long and bold.
Stars shining so bright,
Oh what a beautiful sight.
The wind's howling at the door,
I'm so glad to be indoors.
My bed covers pulled up high,
My hot water bottle roasting hot.
My sister in her cot,
I fall asleep listening to the sounds of winter.

Janet Warke (14)
Coleraine High School

The Coming Of Winter

Awakening that morning, cool and frosty,
Everything had changed.
Mornings no longer warm and hazy,
Now more cool and glistening white.

Walking along, animals snug in their homes,
The last robin sings its song for the day.
Children go home after fun in the snow,
Their rosy cheeks numb with cold.

The hustle and bustle quietens down,
There is an eerie silence unlike no other.
Everything is dead and in slumber.

The smell of cooking sweeps me into a dream,
The warmth of the fire wraps around me like a cloak.
The winter is coming,
No longer the sweet music of birds humming.

Nicola Platt (14)
Coleraine High School

Christmas Time

As I walk through the snow
I hear the crunches of the grass as I go.
I see a little red robin, perched on a wall,
Amongst the glistening snowflakes as they fall.
Inside Mum's baking a Christmas pud,
Oh, boy it looks and smell so good!
In the living room stands our Christmas tree,
Its glowing lights make me smile with glee.
There're cards from family and friends on the door,
And under the tree there's presents galore.
All waiting to be opened on Christmas day,
Where two thousand years ago in a manger a baby king lay.

Cheryl Mairs (14)
Coleraine High School

Peace

This world full of war she enters,
Through the warm and dazzling sun.
Her crystal clear blue eyes
Won't hide any deep, dark secrets.

Her full red lips and warm, wide smile
Turn hearts of stone to hearts of gold.
With her long brown hair that ripples like the ocean,
She sends an air of tranquillity.

Her rosy cheeks upon that fair complexion
Glow like the midday sun.
A long and silky smooth white gown
Folds neatly around her elegant image.

This world that was and is full of war,
Can be changed with one simple step.
If only people would cooperate
And take the hand of peace.

Jenna Watt (13)
Coleraine High School

The Coming Of Christmas

The cold, icy wind cutting through each person
Their breath turning white as they walk
The puddles on the ground are frozen
Giving the sign that the Ice Queen is back
The glittering glint of frost on the ground
The soft subtle snowflakes fall onto the noses
Of the cars as they pass through the Queen's kingdom
The twinkling lights of the Christmas tree
Reflect off the icicles for you and me.

Kirsty Speers (14)
Coleraine High School

Walked Through Winter

Walked across the crusted grass through the frosty air,
The robin saw me, gave me a gold-rimmed glare.
Walked towards the twinkling star, high up in the ebony sky,
Wind whistled past me and flew on by.
Walked through the murky hills where the crunching snow lay deep,
The stark, pointed, icy branches were ready to weep.
Walked along the frozen pond, a light reflected pale,
Shadows gloomed above me as if they were real.
Walked upon the midnight hills, above the twinkling town,
Snowflakes fluttered past me to settle on the ground.
Walked down into the place of glittering lights,
Where the people slept at peace that night.
Walked through the misty, tranquil streets,
Stopped outside my home, but who was I to greet?
Walked through winter - through its mystery and grace,
Searched for a different world, for a better place.

Hannah Harkness (14)
Coleraine High School

The Coming Of Summer

The warm summer sun is shining bright
Keeping us hot and bringing us light
The happy children coming home from school
Changing to shorts and T-shirts to keep them cool
The pretty bright flowers are all in bloom
Giving off a sweet perfume
At the beach the cool blue sea
And warm sand - it's the place to be
Sausages and burgers on the barbecue
Ready for eating just for me and you!

Laura McKinney (14)
Coleraine High School

The Beauty Of Winter

A white blanket of snow lay upon the ground,
A gentle chilling wind blew through the air,
There was a peaceful stillness with no sound,
All the trees stood motionless, frozen and bare.

The heavens above were the shade of grey-blue,
Over the fields the snowflakes softly dust,
The sky darkened to an indigo hue,
Trees swayed in rhythm with the gentle gust.

Windows radiate warmth and light to a world so cold,
And every Christmas tree glints with silver and gold,
And the spirit of love descends to Earth,
Which reminds us of the sacred birth.

Lauren Norris (14)
Coleraine High School

Peace

The quietness has come,
No quarrels to be had,
Free from all disturbance,
Not to last.
Relaxing on the grass,
Above I see,
No turbulent clouds,
The feeling of ease.
No hustle or bustle,
Not a sound heard,
A feeling of freedom,
The passing of a bird.
That snow-white creature,
The dove flies by,
To have this feeling,
Ah peace!

Lisa McNabb (13)
Coleraine High School

The Coming Of Hallowe'en

Children disguised as various creatures
Leaving out none of the features.
Ghosts, vampires, zombies and witches
Every black cats' whiskers twitches.
The night of the luminous full moon
When the werewolves appear so soon.
Looking up at a clear dark velvet sky
As you hear all the mortals cry.
Youngsters go trick or treating
And all the monsters creep around peeking.
Broomsticks, garlic, fake spiders and bats
Devil's staff, black capes and a witch's hat.
All these things
To make you cringe.
Candy-corn, toffee apples and sweets
All everyone really wants is treats.
Then someone plays a dirty trick
It scares you so much you want to be sick.
Parties happening in all the streets
Nobody cares if they dance like freaks.
This mysterious night of extravaganza
Is of course the 31st of October . . .
It's *Hallowe'en!*

Tracy Carson (14)
Coleraine High School

Summer Sunshine

Happy hot holidays here we come!
Lots of heat and fun in the sun.
Sizzling sausages on the barbecue,
The zing of luscious lemonade too!
No need to work, we can relax,
Stop to smell the roses and enjoy them to the max.
Sunbathing on the beach and splashing in the sea
All hold happy memories for me!

Catherine Morrison (14)
Coleraine High School

Rain

I look outside and see the rain,
The sky looks as if it's in pain.
The sky is getting cloudier
And I am getting sleepier.

As I lie in my bed
With thoughts running through my head,
I hear the pitter-patter of the rain
Bouncing off my windowpane.

The next morning when I wake up,
I go downstairs and lift my cup.
As I fill it up with milk,
I see the cloudy sky looks like silk.

I put on my coat and go outside
And from the rain I try to hide,
Jumping in puddles as I go,
The route to school seems so slow.

Nicola Stirling (13)
Coleraine High School

The Coming Of Christmas

As the feather - like snowflakes fall,
From the dark mysterious sky,
People below travel from door to door,
Singing and laughing more and more,
Children are out in the frosty day,
Playing excitedly in the soft, white snow.
Others are in decorating their trees,
Children are starting their letters with 'Please'
Inside the warm home, where it sparkles all colours
Holly, tinsel and mistletoe hang,
With neatly wrapped presents waiting under the tree,
Everyone is dancing with glee.

Helen Caldwell (14)
Coleraine High School

Kindness

A chubby, round woman
With a cat upon her lap
Sat in a corner
Taking a nap.

She has small, round glasses
And rosy-red cheeks,
Very curly hair and can sleep for weeks.

When she opens her eyes
You can see
They are bright blue
And as beautiful as can be.

She puts her hand in her pocket
Then stares at you
And then brings out
A sweet or two.

Naomi Rea (13)
Coleraine High School

The Coming Of Autumn

Summer is going, leaving nothing behind
Yet I will not miss it at all in my mind
As when the next season comes from out of the night
It will bring different colours to everyone's sight

Brown, yellow, gold and red
All lying on the pavement dead
And with the sound of the crunch as I walk
And the gentle breeze with its soothing talk

The birds at the fruit, singing softly to each other
The chestnuts on the trees for me and my brother
The sunsets at night bring a red glow to the sky
When this coming season flies right by.

Heather Ralph (14)
Coleraine High School

Butterflies

Butterflies can be shy
Instead of coming down,
They stay up high,
As they fly in the sky.

All different colours
As they flap their wings.
They're not like the others,
Such beautiful things.

They're playful creatures
That flutter around
That's all they seem to do
I've never seen them on the ground.

Red, green, yellow or blue,
Which is you favourite?
It's up to you!

Annie Hegarty (13)
Coleraine High School

My True Love!

As he strolls up to see me,
With his head held high.
His strong arms reaching out,
As he pulls me near.
With his warm, welcome smile
And his dazzling, blue eyes.
He's tall, dark and handsome,
With a big heart of gold.
When I hear his voice,
My knees go so weak.
I love him,
I need him,
Always close to my heart!

Linzi-Jane Black (13)
Coleraine High School

Anger

Anger is a woman
Tall and strong
Shaking her fiery red curls
She condemns both right and wrong

On metal tipped shoes
Sharp and quick her walk
With a diamond edged voice
She strikes fear when she talks

Smouldering dark brown eyes
Pierce deep into your mind
She has never known a love
Of any shape or kind

Her never-ending fury
Shall torment her all her days
Anger embeds itself deeper
In all she does and says

Deep inside there is a burning
Hot as Hell
Anger is her sickness
And she never will be well.

Esther Alleyne (13)
Coleraine High School

The School Gym

Wooden floors, creaking and gleaming
So cold, so hard, so seemingly demon
The PE class we'll follow her in
And so we're started, let Hell begin

White trainers screech as they ruin the floor
The sounds echoing and bouncing, escaping then more
The teacher bellows, sending chills to my core,
Please let me out, let me through the door.

Abby McCracken (13)
Coleraine High School

Love

Imagine love as a person
What he would look like
Who would he be
A twinkle in his eye
As he looks at me

A heart so big
So genuine and pure
An overwhelming feeling
Feeling with no cure

To hold love in your arms
And never let him go
The joy of just being with him
You'll never ever know

My love sounds a little clichéd
But with all my heart it's true
Cupid put us together
He stuck our hearts with glue

So when you find a love like this
Keep him until the end
Lovers aren't just soulmates
They're your closest ever friends.

Kirsty Steele (13)
Coleraine High School

Pedal Bin

You're a garbage-eating monster.
There seems to be no limit to how much you eat.
You make no noise as you swallow.
Your mouth is a big, gaping, black hole.
Your body shines when the light hits it.
But you usually sit in the shadow of the corner.
You stay still until you are offered something.
You attack! Then go silent again,
Waiting for your next victim.

Catherine Lamont (13)
Coleraine High School

Beauty

With long, golden, silky hair,
Twinkling eyes that shine so bright,
A nose that is so perfect in shape
As she walks across the hall with pride.

A smile that gleams across the room,
For one moment this life's worth living.
Her features light up like an angel from Heaven,
Spreading joy in this miserable world.

With a fine figure and slender limbs,
Like a ghost she glides across this place.
If any woman was as beautiful as her
She would spread peace and love to anyone she knew.

Helen Aiken (13)
Coleraine High School

My Swing

Swinging on my swing high and low
Up flying with the birds I go
The wind is blowing in my hair
And the swing is creaking, but I don't care.

As I fly up and down
I look round and see my town
I kick out my legs then bring them in
Then I decide I want to spin

I twist the swing to make it turn
As I get faster my stomach starts to churn
I get faster and faster and begin to feel ill
I jump off my swing and the world becomes still.

Hannah Hough (13)
Coleraine High School

Beauty

Her tall, graceful, honest posture
Her sapphire sparkling eyes
With teeth as white as falling snow,
Shown off in a perfect smile.

Her long, silky, golden hair
Blows gently in the breeze,
Cascading down her elegant shoulders
The scent blows all around.

She walks tall and confident,
Her legs so long and thin
With skin so tanned and baby-soft,
But her beauty lies within.

Deborah Morrell (13)
Coleraine High School

Early Winter

The bare branches tremble and I watch the last leaf fall,
The cruel wind laughs as it whistles with delight.
A selfish grey sky swallows the sorrowful sun before us all
And the dying trees bow despairingly at their plight.

The cold, hard ground beneath my feet,
Is caked in bitter frost.
The last bird searches for something to eat,
But hopeful thoughts of flowers or life have been lost.

I pray to see a fruitful tree, in blossom with its leaves,
Or a young lamb skipping in a field.
March can save us from this endless death, a new world she weaves.
Eventually stubborn Jack Frost will yield.

Lauren Pratt (13)
Coleraine High School

Motion!

I like the never-ending motion of the sea
In summer mild and gentle - in winter wild
And the swaying motion of the branches on the big tree
Near my window where the breeze is soft and mild.

I love the freedom motion when I swing
Up and down and back and forwards on my swing
I could sit and swing and swing I'm sure forever
If no one bothered me with some other silly thing

Ballet dancing is so very graceful
I'd like to do it - indeed I've tried a lot
But from what I've heard aloud from friends and family
'Poetry in motion' - no I'm not!

Fireworks time is just around the corner
With bangs and sparklers, rockets large and small
I love the loud commotion they all bring
But my poor dog doesn't like them - not at all.

I comfort him when I see emotion
Of fear or sadness in his big brown eyes
But soon his tail is wagging and he's happy
I'm glad 'cause I don't like doggie sighs.

Sarah Acheson (13)
Coleraine High School

Jealousy

As she walks by, I take a glance
at this figure of a woman, in the shadows of the night,
her long, black, wavy hair hangs down upon her face,
her smooth, pale skin reflects the moonlight.

Her piercing green eyes, sparkle like emeralds,
even when her coldest look is given.
Her long, black, fluttery eyelashes
keep her true nature hidden.

The tall, thin figure glides on,
her wonderful green gown, dragging on the ground.
Then suddenly something catches her interest,
a clinking, jingling sound.

Like a gleaming bright light she glows green,
envious of the sight she sees,
someone with treasures, that she often did seek,
this was the moment to seize.

She strikes, pouncing like an eagle on its prey,
taking what she wants without delay,
she takes off down an alley, disappearing from sight,
without words, without a sound, on this clear, cool night.

Hayley Mearns (13)
Coleraine High School

Summer

Hooray! At last the summer's here,
I've looked forward to this all year!
Now that all the work is done,
It's time to really have some fun!

Long summer days spent on the Strand,
Or a lovely cruise up the River Bann.
Don't forget the suntan cream,
This really feels like a wonderful dream!

Going down the prom to meet my friends,
Discussing all the latest trends.
Eating ice cream in Morelli's café,
To cool us down on a hot summer's day.

Two weeks we'll spend in sunny Spain,
Feel the heat as we get off the plane.
Swimming in the Mediterranean sea,
Summer is really the life for me!

Rachael Thompson (13)
Coleraine High School

Envy

When she walks into a room darkness follows,
Her cold, green, watery eyes could kill in one glance
They are underlined in dark, black circles,
Her long black hair hangs like rats' tails from her head,
She roams the street, alone, late at night,
If she sees someone better off than herself she frowns,
She clasps their shoulders with her long, bony hands
And sucks out their life with her thin, red lips,
The victim falls dead on the floor,
She's a murderer but feels no guilt
And will be back to do the same tomorrow night!

Catherine Martin (13)
Coleraine High School

Sparky My Dog

I am woken by the door of the kitchen opening,
By the mother of the house.
She says, 'Hello,' and pats my head
And then I know it's time to be fed.

I'm black and brown
And never frown.
I do what I'm told.
I'm as good as gold.

I always get a lot of treats.
I'm the envy of the streets.
I go for a walk every night
And when I come back they turn out the light.

I love my family.
They always cuddle me.
I hope they'll never give me away,
Because I really want to stay.

Nicola Claire Bacon (13)
Coleraine High School

The Sea

The shore comes in
The shore comes out
People swim
People play
Boats sailing on the water
Having races and having fun
Dogs playing fetch
Seagulls overhead
The sun in the distance
Reflecting the water
What a pretty sight,
The horizon.

Tara McLaughlin (13)
Coleraine High School

The Sea

A dismal and depressing sea
Thunderous breakers crashing against the rocks
I feel its savage waves break when they reach the sand
Lurching forward
Thrashing anything in its way.

The icy wind howls and echoes in my ear.
Spray is flying hither and thither
A shiver runs down my spine
Goosebumps are fast appearing on my skin.

Storm clouds are gathering
The dark leaden sky is bleak
Lightning lashes across the sky
I can hear thunder trembling in the distance.

The clammy air makes me feel uneasy
My head is spinning
My stomach aches
What is happening to me?

I can still hear the waves
The threatening thunder and see the lightning
Now there are torrents of rain
I'm soaked through and through.

Catherine Paul (13)
Coleraine High School

Silence Haiku

Silence tastes like fear,
Seconds tick as minutes fall,
Pin, by pin, dropping.

Cate Cameron-Mitchell (11)
Coleraine High School

The BCG Vaccine

Though some would rather run a mile,
The pupils walked in single file,
Heading to the dreaded room
Where most would have to face their doom.

Of course, there were a lucky few
Whose six pricks stamp was still in view.
They wouldn't have to meet the fate
For which the others now stood in wait.

For in that room three nurses waited
And the unlucky pupils' breath was bated
Because those nurses gave the BCG
To those whose stamp you couldn't see.

The pupils a few at a time, were admitted
But some of them quite badly fretted.
They burst into tears and rang their mum
Telling her she had to come.

When everyone had finally been injected
They said, 'It wasn't what I'd expected.
I thought I'd be in loads of pain,
But I could go through it all again!'

Julie Stockton (13)
Coleraine High School

Autumn Haiku

Yellow, brown and red,
Autumn time has come again,
There's cold in the air.

Joy Cochrane (11)
Coleraine High School

A Kiwi

Skins feels rugged and hairy,
Like a grubby man on the streets,
Unshaven and stubby,
Harsh and churlish,
Appearance, unattractive and scruffy.

But, inside the fruit is radiant and cheerful,
Like a merry girl on a summer's day,
Striking and dynamic,
Full of life and exuberance,
Appearance, alluring and glorious.

Its dull exterior can't compare,
With its glowing bright green inside.
A little band of brown seeds around the white centre,
Lines like rays of light streaming from it,
Tastes sour but surprisingly sweet.

Rebekah Robinson (13)
Coleraine High School

Our Dog Meg

Our family pet is a dog.
Sometimes she sleeps like a log.
Meg is only four years old
And she can certainly be bold.

She greets me with a lick on the face
But our Meg also likes her space.
Her coat is black and very scruffy
And that's what makes our dog lovely.

She loves going out for walks
And also plays with rocks.
Dogs are always man's best friend
So I think Meg is a real gem.

Victoria McQuilkin (13)
Coleraine High School

Ughhh School Again

I find myself
Hitting the alarm again
Praying that it was
Saturday all over again.

Fighting for
The bathroom again
Driving the ten miles
To school again.

Collecting books from my
Locker again
Listening to a lecture
In assembly again.

Classes beginning at
Ten past nine again
Lots of homework
And tests again

Forgetting books and
Homework again
Being told off by
The teachers again

Running to catch
The bus again
Scrambling to get
A seat again

Arriving home late again
Spending a lot of time on homework again
Crawling to my bed again
Telling myself to
Wake up again.

Katie Leighton (13)
Coleraine High School

A Recipe For Happiness!

Two large heaped tablespoons of TV.
One tablespoon of playing with my dog.
Add a bar of chocolate for sweetness.
A dollop of a long lie-in.
A bowl of my mobile phone.
Mix together.
Pour in one pint of my family.
Then add two cupfuls of shopping.
Bake in the summer sun.
Sprinkle some spending time with my friends.
Then chop up my favourite film
And there you go a perfect recipe
For *happiness!*

Catherine Clarke (13)
Coleraine High School

Apple

The first bite is crunchy and juicy
The sweet sensation tickling my tongue
A glossy red colour with mixtures of green, orange and yellow
It feels hard, as hard as a nail
It looks refreshing, refreshing to smell and to eat
Round and smooth
Gentle
Its core is hard and tough to eat
The seeds are a dark brown colour like coffee beans
The apple is tempting
The forbidden fruit.

Amy McPeak (13)
Coleraine High School

Bubbles

They make me feel happy, excited and joyful inside.
Disappointment comes when nothing appears,
Curiosity when you don't know what rainbow-marbled colours
Are going to shine.
Salmon-pink turning to gold,
Gliding through the changing colours of the sky.
A pocket of air trapped is inside this glove of colours,
Gently wafting on a light breeze.
My imagination runs wild inside my head
As the floating bubbles make me relax.
They shine and reflect, shimmer and glide through the sky,
Trembling as they come out of the bottle.
Delicate little bubbles soaring and spinning around the room,
Sooner rather than later the bubbles burst
And with them goes the time of relaxation.
Bang! Back I come into reality.

Charis Wray (11)
Coleraine High School

An Empty Space

This emptiness is filling me
I wonder what it is
It could be that he left me
Actually I know that it is

You said you loved me
And you wanted me
But it seems to be
That you were just using me

You never realised
How much you mean to me
I love you, your kiss,
Your eyes, your lips.

Jade Warwick (13)
Coleraine High School

Strawberries

The summer season,
Starting in July,
First green, yellow and unripe,
Then rosy, red and happy,
Grown in rows,
Which are long, slim and green,
With red specks here and there,
As time goes on more and more appear.
They are picked at the top,
By the short, sturdy stem,
Which is surrounded by little green leaves.
That textured feel,
On the outer coat,
Feels like imprinted dots,
Though it's actually the seeds.
Split it in half
And peer inside,
A red juicy flesh,
That is ill at the top - coloured pale white.
A fruit rich with flavour,
A taste that lingers in your mouth.

Hilary Cameron (13)
Coleraine High School

Seasons

The summer breeze through the trees
Is something that really makes me pleased.

Autumn is near and now I fear
That late nights are here.

Winter has come and now we have fun
Building snowmen with big fat tums.

Spring is here and new life has come
New lambs in fields and daffodils like the sun.

Olivia Smith (13)
Coleraine High School

New Girl

'Ah' sighs the girl who stands alone in the playground.
Look at all the people having fun outside
Oh how I wish to have one friend.
But no one knows me I'm just the 'new girl',
Some people look, others stare,
They think I have no feelings
Well I do.

Look at the girl who stands alone in the playground
I'd like to make friends with her but I don't know how,
Maybe she doesn't want any friends,
Maybe she likes to be on her own.

Look at the girl over there playing by herself
Maybe I'll try and play with her
On my way over I feel kind of excited
Maybe I'll have a new friend, yes maybe
Oh I'm nearly there,
Ding! Ding! Ding!
The bell has gone.

Emma Bannister (12)
Coleraine High School

Colour Isn't Everything

He stood alone, discriminated and hurt,
I watched from a distance,
They threw things at him, called him names.
He looked tearful and sad,
I knew why.
I could see, I felt horrified.
He stretched out his arm, I saw bruises and cuts.
I turned away, couldn't bear to watch
And all I heard from the distance was . . .
'Negro, Negro.'

Yasmin Flatt (12)
Coleraine High School

My Disaster Holiday

Me and my mum went to London,
My cousin and auntie too.
At the time we thought it a good idea,
But it was too good to be true.

First, we got the wrong airport,
Which made us very late.
We had to charge to the check-in desk
And find the right gate.

We left the plane and got our baggage
And got on the Underground,
But travelling along the Victoria Line,
Another mistake was found.

We should have been on the Central Line,
But our tube was going the opposite way.
The day was getting worse and worse
And our hotel was miles away.

When we eventually found it,
We weren't a happy bunch.
We cheered up quite a bit, though,
When we unpacked after lunch.

My auntie found that her suitcase,
Wasn't the one she'd packed.
We thought it was hilarious,
But she nearly had a heart attack!

Worse was still to come, though,
When her suitcase had been found.
Because Cuba is too far away,
To go on the Underground!

Despite the stress and all the fear,
I can't wait to go again next year!

Leona Blair (12)
Coleraine High School

Portstewart!

Portstewart at night
Is a pretty sight.
It is dark,
But it's lively you see.

Inside the homes,
Where lots of people roam,
The lights are on.
Can you see?

People driving cars
Never leave their doors ajar
And never leave the windows open, either.

Portstewart at day,
Is a different array.
For we need no lights,
Anymore.

It is not too dark,
For a walk in the park.
See the people on the street,
Meeting together again.

People walk their dogs
And they throw logs
And it's all done on the beach,
Beside the sea.

It's getting darker
And the children are all smarter.
Because they have just spent hours at school,
Big bore!

So that is the end,
Of this great big trend.
Until another day!

Shauna Bratten (12)
Coleraine High School

Summer, Autumn, Winter And Spring

It's summertime,
Look at those beautiful trees,
Those lime-green leaves,
The sun's so bright and warm.

It's autumn time once more,
Look at those leaves.
They are getting brown oh no oh dear,
Look there's a conker over there
Better pick it up.

It's wintertime again
The leaves have all gone
On what was once a beautiful tree
But it's snowing, that makes it up.

It's springtime again
Look at those cute little lambs.
But look the leaves are back on the trees again
Such a beautiful sight
Those lime-green leaves and a bright blue sky.

Cathy Callaghan (12)
Coleraine High School

Grapes

Raindrops of spring.
In a cluster together,
Silky smooth, ripened flesh,
Smells fresh, like spring weather.
Green like the grass, oval in shape,
A lust for picking.
Such temptation to taste!
A centre of succulence
And sweet juices inside,
So luscious and delicious . . .
That there's none left to hide!

Jenna Purcell (13)
Coleraine High School

Darkness

I wait by the water's edge,
Sad eyes reflected in the moonlight,
Sadness surrounds me with untamed rage.

Imprisoned in the cold dark night,
Where only dangers lurk in the shadows,
I shudder at the fear of a bite.

I gaze at the moon that once was beautiful,
But now, looks like a graveyard,
Which is, I guess, more suitable.

The shadows come nearer,
My heart beats faster,
As the day becomes clearer.

The shadows slowly coil round my fingers,
The moon is nearly gone,
The sun has come, and my spirit, in silence, lingers.

Stephanie Craig (12)
Coleraine High School

Teachers

Teachers always seem to bore
Till we're sleeping on the floor
Their eyes are like hawks searching for prey
And they hang on every word we say.

When it comes to tests they think we've revised
Are we pulling the wool over their eyes?
They say you'll pass with flying colours
Like all your sisters and your brothers.

Well it's about time we've had our say
We go on strike from today
As the war on teachers carries on
We hope and pray tomorrow they'll be gone.

Chlöe Dougan (12)
Coleraine High School

A Few Things Not To Do During An Exam

Exam time's here,
But what not to do?
Well here you go
I've thought of these few.

Don't sit and pick your nose or
Fall asleep during your chemistry practical.
Don't bring a personal radio
And listen to the match.
Don't sit and knit or
Inspect the contents of your ear.
Don't ring your boyfriend and
Don't chew gum to the latest dance tune.

Well that was my few,
Now what about you,
What not would you do?

Olivia Esler (12)
Coleraine High School

My Pets And Me

I sit inside the living room,
My pets love to rub my tummy,
I stick my legs up in the air,
They think I'm cute and funny.

I wait for my pets to come from the bus,
When they see me they make such a fuss,
I eat my food to last me tonight,
I jump on the window sill - Oh! what a height!

Miaow! Miaow! Let me in,
If you don't, I'll make a din.
Ah! that's better, comfy inside,
Oh no! they're coming to hug me,
I'd better go and hide!

Sarah Boyd (13)
Coleraine High School

Ship To America

The eighteenth century was the time,
When words and phrases came to rhyme,
Like flies and fleas and bugs and lice,
Diseased vermin, rats and mice.

We knew what we were heading for,
But even though we were so poor,
We knew the lives awaiting us,
Maybe we should have taken the bus!

But all aboard the ship we went,
Even though I hadn't a cent,
I looked at the bunks and was appalled,
I went to my bed and sat and bawled.

The storms meant we had no dinner,
We grew frail and much thinner,
The oatcakes, I started to get sick of them,
So did the children and the men.

At last we got a breath of fresh air,
After all those weeks of hunger and despair,
We entered America in bright sunlight,
I knew that I'd sleep well that night.

Cherie Gamble (12)
Coleraine High School

Counting Down To Christmas

Christmas time is here again.
Lots of cards to write and send.
Presents wrapped and under the tree,
Twinkling lights to greet you and me.

Christmas cake is iced and ready.
The turkey is being plucked and stuffed.
Stockings are hung and carols are sung.
For tomorrow is Christmas Day.

Laura McFarlane (12)
Coleraine High School

Changing Schools

I've just finished my primary school,
The summer has arrived,
The work has all finished
And I'm going to have a great time.

The summer is over,
The dreaded day has arrived,
I'm starting my new school today,
Today is that day.

School has been going well,
I know my way around now,
The subjects are getting started
And the work is getting good.

I have survived my first month,
So don't be afraid,
We have lots of fun
And we get our work done!

Julianne Hegarty (12)
Coleraine High School

Sports

Running, jumping, swimming, I like it all,
I also love playing netball.
I like running very far,
Someday I'd like to be a star.

It is all really good,
If you don't already play a sport, you should.
Badminton is really cool,
If you don't like it, I think you are a fool.

If your sporting skills are bad,
Do not be sad.
If you just try you could be good,
You could, you could, you could.

Rachel Black (11)
Coleraine High School

Fairies

Do you see them?
Maybe not
They're under the bush,
Or so I thought.

I'm sure I saw
A flicker of gold,
But I've got a vivid imagination,
Or so I'm told.

There goes another and another,
Such small people with wings,
They glow with coloured light
And like natural things.

I know that I'm a dreamer,
A 'wild imagination' they say.
No, I'm very sure I saw them,
Oh, I really hope they stay.

Ilea Hendron (12)
Coleraine High School

The Sea

The sea is like a wild tiger,
Crashing and ripping boats apart.

The sea is like a loving mother,
Giving homes to fish and sea creatures.

The sea is like a big museum,
Storing wreckages of old boats.

The sea is like a great play park,
With children splashing all around.

The sea is like a portrait gallery,
Where we see our reflections in the water.

Sara Wilson (11)
Coleraine High School

Don't Forget Your Head

On a cold winter's day
The young lad jumps on his sleigh.
Bronze with rust and covered in dust,
Forwards he thrusts, he's on his way.

Zooming past cars he now sees stars
As he crashes into a barber's door.
Head spinning, he isn't grinning,
In fact he's crying with pain.

Home he trots, in a strop,
Where he finds his mum in mid chop.
She stops him dead and feels his head,
'Away, away to bed,' she said.

As he awakes full of relief,
He gives a sigh and says this brief.
'Never again shall I omit,
To wear my safety helmet!'

Lauren Hunter (12)
Coleraine High School

Christmas

Children getting excited on Christmas Eve night,
Never stopping to think about the poor children
Who do not get any presents,
Have you ever thought about them?
Many people have not.

The people who have are not just thinking of themselves,
Remember it is not about presents, lights and a tree.

It is not about you or about me,
It is about the poor people and Jesus,
Because if Jesus was not born,
There would be no such things as Christmas.

Sarah Breen (11)
Coleraine High School

Poetry Problems

In English class one morning,
A poem we're asked to write.
I tried all through that evening
And then again next night.

I'm not too bad at spelling.
I can add pennies, cents and dimes.
But when it comes to writing poetry,
I cannot think of rhymes.

I tried and tried and tried,
To end my verses in rhyme.
The more I tried,
The more it seemed to be a waste of time.

Now I fear the time has come,
To put my poem to the test.
I only hope my teacher,
Sees that I have tried my best.

Emerald Owens (12)
Coleraine High School

My Dog Meg

My dog Meg
Is a working pup,
She tries very hard
And never gives up.
Meg rounds up the sheep
And puts them in their pen,
She's far better,
Than any hard-working men.
When Meg is finished working,
She lays down her head,
If you want her to work some more,
You'll find her sniffing round the shed.

Laura Kemps (11)
Coleraine High School

The New Kid

A shy, wandering schoolboy
Walking around clutching his favourite toy.
Snatch! goes the teddy bear,
A small lonely tear.

His teacher's really nice to him,
Her name is Mrs Sim.
She gave him his teddy back
He went and put Ted in his backpack.

The rest of the day was good,
He enjoyed IT as much as he could.
He played with another kid
And really liked the sandpit.

The home time bell rings through the halls,
The children stop and drop their balls.
The boy runs out and grabs his coat,
But forgot about Ted and his little wooden boat.

He ran back in, and just in time,
Another boy tried to steal it, the slime!
Out he went again, 'I had a great day!'
He shouted as he saw his mum and waved.

Suzanne Patton (12)
Coleraine High School

My Kittens

I have two kittens
Who like to play with my mittens.
One is called Socks
Who has white socks.
The other is Marmalade
Who likes to eat marmalade.
They are so cute
Because they are so fluffy and cute.

Claire Wilson (12)
Coleraine High School

Starting School Again

I hear my alarm clock again,
Buzzing at 7am again
Get up to have breakfast again,
To feel completely tired again.

I put on my bottle-green uniform again
Rushing to wash my face again,
To think, *What do I need?* again,
Running to get the bus again.

Walking into school again,
Late for assembly again,
Getting books from my locker again,
Then rushing to class again.

Teachers in bad moods again,
Yelling at us to keep quiet again,
I'm afraid I'll have to say this again
Tomorrow, I'll have to do this all over again.

Cathy McAlonan (13)
Coleraine High School

Loneliness . . .

Miserable and unhappy,
Hopelessness and despair,
Rejected and excluded
No one seems to care.

My heart is feeling heavy,
Alone and terrified,
An outcast in this empty world
Emptiness inside.

I feel like I'm deserted,
I'm feeling all alone,
Can anybody hear me?
Is there anyone at home?

Shauna Platt (11)
Coleraine High School

Individual Medley

I'm called for the next race
My heart begins to pace,
The timer checks his clock,
I mount the diving block.

The starter calls, 'Get ready,'
I try to keep quite steady,
If I dive before the gun,
The race will not be won.

We're off! It's butterfly!
One length of this. Oh why
Did they invent this killer stroke?
It must have been a joke.

Backstroke after the first turn,
I already feel my limbs burn,
Don't know when I'll hit the wall,
That's the problem with back crawl!

Push off the wall. It's breaststroke,
This is now my favourite stroke,
I begin to speed up the pool,
I'm second. First. This is cool!

Front crawl is the final lap,
The crowd begin to cheer and clap.
But my energy is getting low,
I'm beaten by half a metre or so.

Better luck next time!

Catherine Stewart (11)
Coleraine High School

Term Begins *Again!*

I find myself sleeping in again,
Rushing to get ready for school
Again.

My sister takes ages in the bathroom again
And I nearly missed the bus
Again.

Form teacher calls the role again,
While we sit chatting away
Again.

We're back working in class again,
But I've forgot some of my books
Again.

Well school is finally over again,
And I'm sitting on the bus
Again.

Loaded up with homework again
And I'm getting into bed
Again.

I finally get to sleep again,
Then I wake up in the morning again,
To find that I've overslept,
Again!

Rachael McKeeman (13)
Coleraine High School

Moonlight

On that dark night
When the moon was shining diamond-white
And twinkling like a crystal in the sky

The world was asleep
And didn't give a peep
Unaware of the planets moving in the sky

The silence was broken
By the wind's howl but not awoken
Were the people tucked up in bed

The moon would soon say goodbye
As the sun rose in the sky
And the morning began to awake

But we'll never forget
That scene and that set
And the night that the moon came alive.

Lauren McCollum (11)
Coleraine High School

Motions Of Nature

Have you ever seen the gracefulness
Of a white dove in flight?
It flies up high o'er vales and hills
From the light of dawn till the starry night

Have you ever seen the beauty
Of a fish swimming in the sea?
It swims with such a gracefulness
I wish that fish was me

Every animal has a motion
Graceful, elegant, true
I wish I could be like that
And I think that you would too.

Naomi Dorrans (12)
Coleraine High School

An Autumn Walk

Walking
Through the forest
Leaves
Falling from the trees
Crunching underfoot

Wind
Blowing through the branches
Rain
Bouncing on the ground
I'm getting wet

Squirrels
Happily gathering nuts
Birds
Leaving, flying south
Busy, busy season.

Clare Taylor (11)
Coleraine High School

Autumn Day

I looked out of my window,
To see the scattered leaves,
Lying on the ground,
The trees all bare.

The wind blows through the empty street,
There's no one out there to meet,
The trees blow wild,
With the whistling of the wind.

The leaves all scattered,
Makes the street look cluttered,
The evening gets dark
And I hear not a single bark.

Tamsin McKissick (12)
Coleraine High School

Seasons

Early spring, when it's still quite cold
'Come back, come back,' the swallows are told.
Late spring, when flowers start growing on trees
'It's time to fly,' buzz the bees.

All through summer it's nice and warm
And there's not a sign of rain or storm.
In the summer everyone has fun
And everyone is joyful under the sun.

Early autumn, the leaves start falling
And the wind gradually starts calling.
Late autumn, when most leaves are dead
Some animals get ready for bed.

Lovely winter, when it usually snows
'Chirp, chirp, chirp,' the robin goes.
At New Year's Day we count down to one
And hope we'll have a new year of fun.

Rui Wang (11)
Coleraine High School

Waves

The winds whip up
Crashing down on the sea
A storm has begun.

The sea grows angry
Chasing towards the jagged rocks
Snow-white horses rise from the deep
Lashing out at the stones
With all their strength.
Meeting only briefly they return to the sea.

The wind dies down.
The sea sleeps softly.
Calm has returned.

Beth Eustace (12)
Coleraine High School

Autumn

Leaves are falling
Falling to the ground
Wind is howling
Blowing all around

Hear the robins singing
Singing with all their might
See the swallows fly
Far, far away

The nights are getting longer
The days are getting shorter
The weather is getting colder
The wind is blowing harder

The trees are bare
The ground is damp
It's that time of year again
Autumn has arrived.

Sarah Robinson (11)
Coleraine High School

Time In Motion

Left, right, to and fro,
Never fast and never slow.
Left, right, at a constant pace,
Going nowhere nor in a race.

Left, right, in the night,
Swinging gently till daylight.
Left, right, all day long,
Moving to a silent song.

Left, right, all the time,
Every hour we hear it chime,
Left, right, tick-tock,
Moving hands on the clock.

Rachel McGowan (12)
Coleraine High School

An Autumn Morning

The leaves are falling crisp and brown
It's an autumn morning.
The sky is heavy, the clouds dark grey.
The birds are looking for a place to stay.
The farmer's in the fields till late
Because it's nearly harvest time.
There's a chill in the air
But I don't dare go out without my coat.
I'll be like a boat being tossed about in the sea by the fierce wind.
It's started raining
If I don't hurry I'll start complaining.

The leaves sit there blowing in the breeze,
They once were green but now are brown.
They once were young and full of life,
But now they're old and weary.
Brown and wrinkled,
They hang on the tree,
Thinking of spring and summer.
A strong wind blows
They're gone,
They flutter gently to the ground
And lie there among the rest.

Lori Shirlow (11)
Coleraine High School

Snowflakes

Elegantly they drop from the top of the clouds.
As they gracefully fly through the sky.
They come in all different shapes and sizes.
None would be the same shape as another.
They are as white as angels.
It is cold when they are about.
We still look out though to see them.

Diane Clyde (11)
Coleraine High School

School

Teachers scribbling on the board with squeaky chalk,
Clocks go tick-tock.
School bags zipping,
Files clicking
Pencils clattering,
Children chatting.
The start of another day,
I think I'll go my own way.

Now it's home time,
Faces shine.
Cars tooting,
Children shouting.
Coats ruffling.
Feet trotting.

And people think I'm supposed to study
With all this going on!

Niamh Owens (11)
Coleraine High School

The Gymnast

With fairy grace the gymnast
Steps along the bench,
Nimbly she flips
Landing in an amazing handstand,

A silent crowd in wonder sits,
Gazing with awe at her still,
The routine complete,
She sweeps gracefully to her seat,

As the crowds applaud
The next competitor.

Vivien Lyons (11)
Coleraine High School

Mysterious Mothers

From behind a branch two beady eyes peep.
The Senegal bushbaby awake from sleep.
A bushy tail and four-clawed feet,
Going out only at night to feed.

The young sleep in their cosy nest.
Their mother thinks this place is best.
So no predators can think, *there's a meal for me.*
If that were the case they would no longer be.

Out of the nest her wide eyes peer.
She is careful but has no fear.
She needs to gather food for her young.
Bushbabies love tree gum.

Time for her and her young to sleep.
Until again it is time to peep
Out of the cosy dry straw nest.
But until then it is time to rest.

Lisa Douglas (11)
Coleraine High School

The Sun And The Sunset

Morning time, I look outside my window
The low sun blazes into my eyes.
It's autumn!

The leaves trickle to the ground,
Crispy, red and yellow,
What a beautiful sight.

At the end of the day,
The sun sinks slowly, yellow, red and orange
Into a fiery sunset.

Rebecca Holley (11)
Coleraine High School

My Horse

I ride my horse every day,
I feed him apples and a bale of hay,
He likes to gallop through the park,
I put him to bed when it's dark.

His name is Spot,
He eats a lot,
I put his saddle on his back
And ride him down the winding track.

When I look up and see the sky,
I take him to the park and let him fly,
I take him through the jumping course,
He is a lovely horse.

He loves to jump and play about,
We hear the people in the park shout,
'Come watch this horse, come see him gallop,'
As he jumps over a wooden pallet.

I bring him back to the stable
And groom his coat until it's smooth,
He's in his bed so nice and neat,
With his blanket at his feet.

Now it's time for me to go to bed
And rest my weary head,
My mum comes in to switch off the light
And say, 'Goodnight.'

Catherine Tweed (11)
Coleraine High School

The Big Match!

I'm warming up before the match,
I'm walking slowly but my heart's pounding fast.
The whistle blows and we take kick-off,
I'm so scared of doing something wrong and I just feel I don't belong.
The temptation is burning inside of me to race right up the pitch
And let my feelings free.
From Jimmy to Timmy and he passed to me.

I'm feeling scared but the crowd's cheering for me.
My spirits arise and I'm not scared anymore,
I really wonder if I could score.
It is hard or so they say but I will get a goal someday.
The ball is passed, I'm near the goal.
I'm running quick, I'm running fast,
I wonder if this could be it at last.

I pass to John, he passes back to me,
I really wonder if this could be.
I take a shot and what a chop.
The goalie's running but that ball won't stop.
So there it is in the back of the net and that's a goal I won't forget.
I'm really happy and I can't believe that I could ever be so pleased.
So there it is I've got my goal,
So now I think I'll just rest my soul.

Louise Kane (11)
Coleraine High School

Kitty Kitten

K itty kitten begins to wake
I n her basket she begins to move
T winkling eyes looking up at you
T wo ticks and she's up on your knee
E ven when you give her dinner she still miaows
N ails as sharp as can be.

Chantelle Murdoch (11)
Coleraine High School

The Monster Under The Bed

While everyone else was fast asleep,
One little girl was up on her feet,
Though everyone told her to go to bed,
This little girl stayed up instead.

She padded round her bedroom floor,
Hearing croaks and groans and moans and roars.
She sang to try and block out the noise
And woke up the other girls and boys.

This girl decided to face her fears,
This girl had knowledge beyond her years
She lifted the covers to see what it was,
Expecting teeth and paws and lots of claws . . .

She jumped back in great surprise,
She couldn't believe what she saw with her eyes,
It wasn't a monster after all,
But a litter of kittens, meek and small.

Zara Leighton (11)
Coleraine High School

Football

Rangers is my favourite team,
Every time they score I scream,
Rangers are the best
Better than the rest.

Watching football is so cool
If you don't watch it you're a fool
I can't wait to play at school,
I almost know every rule.

I also think Liverpool's OK,
But I'm certain that Rangers will win on the day,
I also can't wait for the day
When Liverpool and Rangers play.

Zoë Browne (11)
Coleraine High School

Ponies

Some ponies are bay
And some are grey
They like treats
But don't give them sweets.

Darcy is a pain
But he has a nice mane,
Of course it's all stray
With hairs of grey,
Which we are told
Is a sign of growing old.

You always hear a wail
While pulling Frosty's tail,
He responds with a kick
And then a big slimy lick.

No matter how bad they can be,
I love them as you see.

Kelly McAfee (11)
Coleraine High School

The Fox

There once was a fox
Who went out late one night
And only had the moon for his light

With his thick bushy tail
Swishing behind him
He pranced and he danced
Till late in the night

And as the dawn broke
Out came the folk
So the fox returned to his den.

Emma McCrea (11)
Coleraine High School

Summertime

If you open your window on a summer's morning what you
might see . . .
A pond with someone in it that looks just like me.
A lonely tree with blossoms, all pink with bits of green
A field full of lambs baaing that makes my face gleam.

The sun has come up to the top of the sky, a sign that means it's noon
I can smell the barbecue cooking, which means I'll be having
lunch soon.

I've finished my lunch now I'm out to stay
I'll play and play until the end of the day.

The sun's gone down and I'm tired out
My friends had me running all about.
I'm going now to bed and hopefully to sleep
It's so quiet now that I can still hear the sheep
Going bleep, bleep, bleep.

Samantha Mairs (11)
Coleraine High School

An Autumn Morning

I wake up in the morning
and what do I see?
Leaves on the ground
crisp as can be.

Squirrels are scuttling
around the town
gathering nuts
that are so brown.

There's nothing better
than autumn cheer
but we'll have to wait
until next year.

Sarah Kirkpatrick (12)
Coleraine High School

The Irish Cup Final

Six hours to go, I'm saying my prayers,
I pull on my shirt and run down the stairs.
My blue and white flag gets minor repairs,
My hands shake so much, my heart pounds.

After my mother invades my space,
I end up with blue and white hair, nails and face.
On the bus to Windsor I take my place.
My voice trembles, my heart pounds.

My chequered flag joins the sea of blue and white,
Big G scores, oh what a sight.
The ref says, 'No,' but he wasn't right.
Such ecstasy, such agony, my heart pounds.

But wait Windsor rumbles Jody scores.
Glen's hearts sink, Coleraine's soars.
'Come on the Bannsiders,' the crowd roars.
So much to lose, my heart pounds.

McCann hits the bar, could this be our day?
But with 20 minutes left, it's time to pray.
'I can't take much more,' I hear my dad say,
Coleraine fans dare to hope, my heart pounds.

At last, at last the whistle sounds.
The Coleraine songs ring round the ground.
Glentoran fans cannot be found,
It's a dream come true, my heart pounds.

Sirri Topping (11)
Coleraine High School

Nightmare

As I'm walking through the woods,
I see a basket full of goods.
I walk closer and into a hole,
Now I'm digging like a mole.
Through the tunnels I will go,
Till I feel the soft wind blow.
There I see a girl so fair,
Whispering, 'Run! I'm your nightmare!'

I do as she says and run,
Then I hear a shot of a gun.
Someone is chasing me and I can see
That their face is full of glee.
Now I'm falling, down and down,
To the ground, to death I'm bound.
There I see the girl so fair,
Whispering, 'Run! I'm your nightmare!'

I woke up shaking
And felt my bed start breaking.
I jumped off as quickly as I could
And stiffly there I stood.
I called for my mum
And then I heard someone hum.
There at the door was the girl so fair
Whispering, 'You can't run! I'm your nightmare!'

Rachel Smyth (11)
Coleraine High School

Close Encounters

Zoos and safari parks they're all the same,
All those animals kept in pain.
Their lonely eyes staring through the bars,
Having been whipped, now with everlasting scars.

Others think it's amazing
Whales, tigers, lions and more.
All day they sit there gazing,
Wondering what it's like out of a cage,
Running wild in the green pasture beyond,
Their energy burning with rage.

Dolphin shows are a great laugh until you know the story,
Of them being beaten or hurt, it all seems a bit gory.
And what a way to end the day
Than to watch the monkeys play
Don't they look so happy,
Yeah right, no way!

So don't go to the zoo again
And look in their sad eyes
Because all it's doing
Is ruining their lives!

Jenna Scobie (11)
Coleraine High School

Bubbles

The beautiful bubbles soar through the sky.
I feel excited, thrilled, happy
And jolly all the time.
I get upset when nothing appears.
A bubble is a marble shape
With such lovely
Colour and detail.
Floating wild and free,
Oh how I long to be that bubble.

Natasha Spence (11)
Coleraine High School

Anna

I was very excited when Anna was born
It was on a Thursday in early morn
Dad came in to tell me the news
He looked rather sleepy and a little confused!

We went to the hospital later that night
And took turns to nurse and hug her tight
She looked very tiny wrapped up in her shawl
But at 8lbs 10, she was not so small!

I helped Mum to bath and get her dressed
It's not long until her clothes are all messed
I like to nurse and sing her a song
But sometimes her nappies - boy do they pong!

She's on her feet and running around
We only get peace when she's sleeping sound
She's funny and tricky, and laughs a lot
She sleeps like an angel tucked up in her cot.

Hazel Ramsey (11)
Coleraine High School

Just One More Step!

Red, yellow, blue, green,
All this gear here to be seen,
They said it would be a breeze,
There was no way I would freeze,
Up I stepped no need to be helped,
Then flight or fright,
Those lights are so bright,

I looked up - I saw that great big smile,
Off I went and knew the catwalk wasn't a mile.

Nicola Andrews (12)
Coleraine High School

Morning

The birds are singing
The alarm clock's ringing
Lying under the covers
Don't want to get up

My mum's shouting
Now I'm pouting
I toss and turn
Don't want to get up

Mum's in my room
Now I assume
She'll open my curtains
Don't want to get up

My dad starts to yell
Now I can tell
I have to get up
Don't want to get up

My head's in a tizz
My hair's in a frizz
I'm late for my bus
I should have got up.

Claire McLaughlin (11)
Coleraine High School

Autumn

The autumn leaves are falling,
The nights are getting dark,
The little robin redbreast,
Searches hungrily in the park,
The trees are changing colour,
Red, yellow and gold,
All the squirrels are gathering nuts
And the hedgehogs are on hold.

Jenna McFaull (12)
Coleraine High School

A New Term

Oh no, there I go,
Going back to that school,
To miss all my favourite shows,

I got heavy black shoes,
In place of comfy trainers
And a knee-length skirt,
To replace my favourite jeans,

The days were short,
But not anymore,
They seem so long,
Why is homework such a bore?

The sun is gone
And so has the fun,
Only grey days left,
Until the end of this term comes.

Rebecca Henderson (13)
Coleraine High School

Bubbles

Rising, rising, rising . . .
Pop!
Off with the bottle's lid.
We're free, soaring like birds.
But then our fantasy ends
Our marbled coat comes off
Our glimmer turns to nothing,
Where are we?
We're back where we started
Rising, rising, rising . . .
Pop!

Robyn Jessica Millar (11)
Coleraine High School

Cats

Running through the fields
So smooth, so sleek
I spy the bird
I want to eat.

Ready to pounce
I crouch down low
Waiting my chance
Here I go!

Push off from the ground
Flying through the air
About to land
The bird, I scare.

Back to her nest
She will fly
Off hunting I go
Again, I sigh.

Jennifer Crossley (12)
Coleraine High School

The Seaside

The sand sliding between my toes,
The waves crashing against the rocks,
It makes me so happy to be in Portrush,
To watch the boats sit in the docks.

The breeze blowing through my hair,
The storm is hitting everywhere.
The fishermen fishing on the rocks,
The seagulls flying in their flocks.

The surfers down with their boards,
The waves are taking control,
The sun's disappearing behind the clouds,
I'm afraid a storm is born.

Emma Wray (12)
Coleraine High School

Off We Go!

In through the door, then onward to my seat.
Be brave, remember I'm no coward.
Up above the bags are packed so neat,
I sit down. We begin to move forward.

I put on my belt, I confess, I don't feel safe.
Ah no, I take it off, my sweets are above my head.
Back on it goes, this time I have more faith
As I watch and take in what is being said.

Everything has gone quiet as I sit and wait.
Suddenly engines roar, I'm pushed back in my seat.
The first part of the journey I truly hate,
The injection of speed makes my heart miss a beat.

I listen to the rumbling of tyres, the air rushing by.
Yes, it's exciting but not really fun.
Up we go, up into the sky.
I sit back and relax and look forward to the sun.

My fear returns and I begin to think, *why*?
Suddenly my smile turns to a frown.
As I gather my thoughts I try not to cry
As I remember that what goes up must come down.

Gillian Wisener (12)
Coleraine High School

Speeding

There once was a woman called Molly,
Who drove to work in a lorry.
She left one morning at a quarter to nine
But a policeman stopped her and asked for a fine.
Molly ignored him and zoomed down the A3,
But lying on the road was a rather large tree.
Molly didn't see it so *crash* she went . . .
And now poor Molly has a lorry so bent.

Lynsey Barr (12)
Coleraine High School

School Bus

I jump on the bus
And grab my seat
I always sit in the back row
Where there's plenty of room for my feet.

The bus starts up
And so does the noise
People laughing everywhere
And the little ones with their toys.

The bus suddenly jerks
As it stops to pick people up
I look out of the window
And see my best mate and her pup.

She hops up on
Her bag in tow
The bus starts again with a jerk
And away to school we go.

Helen Dobbin (12)
Coleraine High School

Energy

Silently waiting, ready to pounce
Flick of the switch, beginning to bounce
Shot from a gun, speeds to the mark
Piercing the air, sounds like spark.

Heat from the sun, light years away
Power from afar lights up the day
Its strength is released, life to the world
Strength without source, bright as a pearl.

No one can see it hidden from view
Gravitational pull falls like the dew
Man tries to control it but doesn't succeed
And nuclear power, where will it lead?

Sarah Minihan (13)
Coleraine High School

Hallowe'en

It's dark and cold
And you shouldn't have to be told
It's Hallowe'en
The time when strange things have been seen.

Ghosts, vampires and pumpkin heads
Have all been sleeping in your beds
Beware! Beware!
You're in for a scare.

Sweets, sweets, glorious sweets
They're the best of all the treats
Trick or treating is a lot of fun
Thinking of all the food for my tum.

I'm in the graveyard walking around
I see a zombie coming out of the ground
I start to run as fast as I can
Watching out for the bogeyman.

Carrie-Lyn Kane (12)
Coleraine High School

Me And My Messy Room

Mum says my bedroom is the messiest it's ever been,
Because she hasn't seen the carpet for ages,
The wardrobe, my clothes have hardly ever seen,
On the floor they build up in stages.

My shelves and surfaces are totally covered,
Displaying all of my favourite belongings,
The walls and door, totally smothered
And the sills piled high with more things.

The mess it just drives Mum mad,
And she's tired of nagging every day,
But she said she can't be sad,
Because she loves me come what may . . .

Emma Neill (13)
Coleraine High School

School Days

On Monday we have music, English and HE
What would make this day great? Just add in some PE!
In music we need recorders, in English all our books
But in HE all we need to know is how to clean and cook!

On Tuesday we've got chemistry, loads of little tests
We've also got IT, it's better than the rest
Last thing on a Tuesday is a single of RE,
But guess what is before it? A period of PE!

First thing on a Wednesday is double geography
Followed closely behind by double biology
Later after lunch it's time for some TD
And what we're making next is a mystery!

Next it is Thursday; soon it's the weekend
Better start organising things to do with my friends
But we're still at school and we've got double PE
Life skills, history and maths not forgetting geography.

The last day of the week, yes yippee hooray!
Teacher's not letting our brains rest, we've got double physics today!
But last thing on a Friday is double art, I know!
And so that ends another week, into town I go!

Gillian Simpson (12)
Coleraine High School

Storm

The sea gently lapped,
The wind rustled through the leaves,
As the cloak of darkness swept
Over the small seaside town.

Children in their beds,
Adults too,
Fishing nets are packed away,
Everything is still.

Rain thudded against the windowpanes,
Waves crashed against the rocks,
The wind howled,
Lightning lit up the skyline.

Fierce winds ruined all things visible
Sea spray flew high in the sky,
Rain turned to hail
And thunder rumbled.

Then suddenly the rain stopped,
The wind died down,
The sea was calm,
The town was still again.

Claire Carson (12)
Coleraine High School

The Teddy Bears

When at night I pretend to sleep,
I can hear small voices squeak.

As they run across the floor,
I can hear them chatter more.

I hear them singing the latest tunes,
Drinking Coke and bursting balloons.

When the sun begins to show,
Back to the toy box they do go.

I hear them tiptoe back to bed,
Golden silence once again.

When in the morning I awake,
I open the toy box just to check.

But they are tucked up safe and sound,
Their faces back to their normal frowns.

All is over for another night,
Until nine o'clock when out goes the light.

Aimée Hamilton (12)
Coleraine High School

In Summer

Summer to me means . . .
No homework,
No homework means no school,
No school means freedom,
Freedom means fun,
Fun means happiness,
Happiness means bliss,
Bliss means luxury,
Luxury means relaxation,
That's how I feel in summer . . . happy, relaxed
and blissful!

Erin McCollum (12)
Coleraine High School

Sunday, Sunday

Sunday, Sunday, what to do?
Shall I clean my room,
Or read that new book?
Mum wants me to clean,
But is she just mean?

Sunday, Sunday, why am I bored?
What can I do to keep me awake?
What's for dinner, is it steak?
Why am I bored, so bored?

Nothing on telly, only my chores,
Oh what a bore
Would it be better on sunnier shores?

Sunday, Sunday, maybe today
Dad will take me somewhere
Different to play.
Boredom is only a thought in your mind,
And you're only as bored, as bored as your mind.

So maybe today I'll take myself off and think that today
I'll just sit back and enjoy all that I have
And think that being bored might not be so bad,
Maybe I'll enjoy all that I have.

Emma Doherty (12)
Coleraine High School

Books

Books, books, books galore,
Read, read, read some more,
Don't stop, don't put it down,
Books, books wear the crown.

Books, books are forever,
Books, books are like hidden treasure,
Books, book are exciting, yes,
Books, books are the best!

Lauren Young (12)
Coleraine High School

The Big Game

There I am standing in the stands
At the Premiership Cup Final
It's Man United v Arsenal
Five minutes to go
One team has to score
Or it will go into penalties
'Come on Man U,' I'm shouting
But will they score?
Oh look a player for Man U
Has been knocked down in the penalty area
The ref has a decision to make
Is it a penalty or not?
And it is. Everything is tense
Will he score?
The ref blows his whistle
The player shoots and he scores!
Yeah! Man U are the Premiership champions.

Clare Reynolds (12)
Coleraine High School

Different Emotions

What is emotion?
Is it anger and hate,
Or excitement and love?
I don't know emotion.

Dark, light,
What is right?
Is it bright
Or is it fright?

We can move,
We can hurt,
We can run,
But where is the fun?

Lauren Kettyle (12)
Coleraine High School

Teachers

Teachers, teachers are wonderful creatures,
You never know what mood they're in.
They could be happy or sad, guilty or mad,
Or have their heads stuck high up in the sky!

Teachers, oh teachers, yes wonderful teachers,
You should be scared of them you know!
So beware of one thing, this wonderful thing,
A teacher on the loose!

Teachers, teachers, they're wonderful creatures,
Their pencils and pens all neat in a pot.
You knock the pot over; you pick the pot up,
Or you will have to pay the consequences; DT.

Teachers, teachers, don't mess with the teachers,
They have wonderful powers you know.
Teachers, teachers, yes wonderful teachers,
Can't live with them, can't live without them!

Hannah Kelly (13)
Coleraine High School

A Recipe For Happiness

1 tablespoonful of TV
A qtr of midget gems
Mixed in with a trip to a massive water park
2 pounds worth of text messages on my new 8310 mobile
And mix well
Sprinkle with the winning ticket of the lottery
Stir in a suitcase of new clothes
Add in the latest gossip
Stir well with some family fun
And there you have it
A recipe for happiness.

Amber Stewart (12)
Coleraine High School

When The Morning Comes

When the morning comes
I raise my head,
Look around,
Then jump out of bed.

I'm getting changed,
The straighteners are on,
My hair is straight,
The moon has gone.

My breakfast is ready,
Hot chocolate and toast,
I'm looking great,
Though I don't mean to boast.

Arrived at school,
Maths is first,
Check over my homework,
My head's going to burst.

Do some revision,
Or I'll fail the test,
On long division,
Then have a rest.

Charlotte Kilgore (12)
Coleraine High School

A Recipe For Happiness

First add a speck of peace and patience
Stir well with summer sunshine
Mix in a smashing spending shopping spree
Pop in some lazy lounging with scrumptious strawberries
Season with chitty, chatty, friendly gossiping
Pour in some courageous karaoke antics
Mix well with jumping, joyful gymnastics
Add a dollop of silly swimming
Bake slowly with relaxing reading
So relax and enjoy.

Laura Doherty (12)
Coleraine High School

Fazzy Wazzy Bear

Yawn, yawn, I'm so tired!
I'm hungry, where's my food?
Here it is, hooray!
And my favourite person too.
Boing, boing, give it me!
Mmm, mmm, mmm!
That was nice grub.
Now you know what's next?
Walkies!
'Wait a minute,' they say.
'Wait a minute.'
I'm bored now,
I'm bored-d-d . . .
Play with me.
'I'm busy,' they say.
Busy doing what?
'You're not the one and only,' they say.
Yes I am!
I'm the best,
I look best and I'm the fastest dog
In the world.'

Gemma Webster (12)
Coleraine High School

Transport

Planes and trains, buses and cars
Some of the transport,
That takes us so far

Ships and lorries, scooters and bikes
So much to choose from,
So much we like.

On roads or on rail, in the air or on sea
Whichever we decide on,
Happy travellers are we.

Rebecca Dysart (12)
Coleraine High School

The Beast Of Ballybogey

Summer arrived and out came the sun
Children out playing, having great fun
Living in the country you expect peace and quiet
Then wild animals were released, causing a riot.

Tales of a puma stalking Bushmills
Sightings reported in fields and on hills
The news of this creature spread far and wide
Even the birds in the sky tried to hide.

The puma's first attack caused great alarm
Panic set in - no sheep was safe from harm
TV cameras and reporters moved in
To be first with the story - they needed to win.

Another attack close to a school
Showed that this puma was nobody's fool
It took a wild animal causing a flap
To finally put Ballybogey on the map.

Summer's now gone and so has the sun
Children kept in, not allowed out for fun
A tourist attraction as good as Loch Ness
No thanks, the puma can go and so can the press.

A massive puma hunt, no sign of success
Angry words spoken - it's all such a mess!
Good luck to the puma in its new habitat
Forever to be known as Ballybogey's big cat.

Julie Magee (13)
Coleraine High School

The Cat And The Rat

There was a cat named Rat.
There was a rat named Cat.

They got their names
From playing chasing games,
Because the cat chased the rat,
And the rat chased the cat,

But then one day
The rat ran away,
A ginger cat found him
And he was called Jim.

Jim was bad,
He was Rat's dad,
And he ate Rat
Instead of Cat!

He didn't know
That he was quite low,
And Rat was a cat
And Cat was a rat.

He was so sad,
He used to be a good dad . . .
Until he killed his son
And now he's left with none!

Elaine Hunter (13)
Coleraine High School

School

Monday morning
Just can't wait,
'Cause it's time for school,
Can't be late.

I get into school
And talk to my friends
About the night before,
The fun never ends!

But then the bell rings
And the teachers walk past
Shouting, 'Go on, get to your class!'

But I'm still thinking about the night before
But now it's off to history,
Oh what a bore!

Jade McCook (13)
Coleraine High School

Styles

Some people have skater styles
Some people have girlie styles

Some people have that see you later style
And some people have curly styles

Some people have punky styles
Some people have hippy styles

Some people have funky styles
And some people have that dippy style

I'm glad everyone doesn't have the same style
'Cause if they did life would so not be worthwhile

Some people think that looking cool is looking the same
Well I think that is rubbish and is so not my game!

Zara McIntyre (13)
Coleraine High School

What People Say To Me All Day

Get up you lazy lump, out of bed
Hurry up and eat your breakfast
Go and get dressed
That's my mum going on and on.

Tidy your room
Feed the ducks
Hurry up or you'll miss the bus
That's my dad going on and on.

Always spell bonjour right
Keep the noise down
Get your punctuation right
That's my teachers going on and on.

Drive the tractor and get those cows
Drive the quad and get those sheep
Come and help me feed the cows
That's my grandpa going on and on.

Heather Porter (12)
Coleraine High School

Buffy

My name is Buffy, I'm a cat,
My owners give me lots of food,
I eat it all so now I'm fat.

I live in a house, not outside,
It is warm and cosy, with a fire,
Or some beds when I'm tired.

My owners say, 'She is a bad cat,'
Just because I climb up curtains,
Or claw at the living room mat.

When I am tired I curl in a ball,
Close my eyes and relax,
But when I wake up I stand tall!

Stephanie Speers (12)
Coleraine High School

From Geography 2 To English 14

Bell rings,
Time for next class,
Pick up things,
Down the stairs.
Past cookery class,
Teacher shouts,
'Not too fast!'
Now up the stairs,
Knees weak,
Slowly in pairs,
Cannot speak.
Along the corridor,
Past the canteen,
Pushing and shoving,
Some people so mean.
I don't understand,
Why they are so keen,
To get to class,
Through the swing doors,
Up *more and more* stairs,
Legs breaking,
Nearly there.
Feet aching,
Not far to go now.
Last three steps
.. . Two, one, yeah!
Finally,
We're here!

Kathryn Dobbin (12)
Coleraine High School

Orders Of The Day

Quickly girls!
Get your books out
Now get those sums right
That's my maths teacher
Going on and on and on and on . . .

Angle your flute up Emma
Now have you been practising. No I'm thinking
And how many beats is a semi-brieve worth?
That's my music teacher
Going on and on and on and on . . .

Bonjour girls
Now what does that mean in English?
Ça va?
And that too
Quel âge as-tu?
That's my French teacher
Going on and on and on and on . . .

Homework out girls
I hope there are no spelling mistakes!
Today's lesson will be on proverbs
That's my English teacher
Going on and on and on and on . . .

Emma Robson (12)
Coleraine High School

What If I Didn't Have To Go To School

As I sit here in my class,
I listen to everyone talking.
If there was pure silence
Then I wonder how it could be.

If I didn't have to go to school,
If I didn't have to get up early to catch the bus,
Just lie in bed all day
In a nice, warm bed.

Now think about how it could be
If you didn't know how to read, write or draw.
The school has taught us to do all these things
So in a way it's not all that bad.

As I look around the English room
All I see are *books, books,* and more books.
Dictionaries, exercise *books,* novels, text *books,*
Oh please don't let me see anymore *books.*

But from my point of view
I think that school is not all that bad
Because you get to do fun things as well,
It's not all that bad.

But I like school,
It's fun,
Especially English.
And I know we'd all like to be off school forever,
But a couple more weeks of holidays,
Should do the trick!

Holly McCullough (13)
Coleraine High School

Shoes

There's all sorts of different shoes,
And I really don't know what to choose,
There's high-heeled and skater shoes,
But I would like a pair with different shades of blue.

You've got the shoes that are chunky and punky,
And then there's the school shoes, they're certainly not funky.
There're pointy-toed shoes, that some people like,
But the shoes in the next verse are the type I'd like.

Vans, Etnies and Converse,
They're the best shoes in the universe.
But I also like some other shoes,
For example Kangaroos.

Naomi Parkhill (13)
Coleraine High School

Flowers

Flowers come in different sizes,
Roses, tulips, buttercups and daises.
Bright colours when the sun rises,
Smelling the pollen makes me hazy.

Purple, orange, yellow and green,
Busy lizzies are pink.
Rainy weather keeps them clean,
I'm sure I saw one wink.

Pollination, fertilisation and germination
Are the stages they go through.
They grow with determination,
In biology we learn what they do!

Jill Oliver (12)
Coleraine High School

A Recipe For Happiness

A large dollop of Gareth Gates,
Two bowlfuls of family fun,
An ounce of 'chilling' with my friends,
A slice of our family pets,
A large spoonful of music,
Add my summer holidays,
And mix in well,
Leave baking in the sun for no more than two hours,
Add a litre of coke,
And a sprinkle of reading,
Seven tablespoons of TV,
70ml of swimming,
A dash of playing the computer,
Serve with a handful of Christmas days,
Pour on all my 11 birthdays (including all my birthday presents),
And there's my recipe for happiness.

Kerry Kilgore (12)
Coleraine High School

Friends

Each of us can be a friend.
We all have best friends or we can have one best friend.
Friends are important people who you can rely on
if you are feeling blue.
Friendship is about hanging out and playing jokes with your mates.
With friends we have to be honest, kind and thoughtful.
Having friends means you can work together, walk and talk
and be at ease with each other.
I treasure my friends.

Vincent McErlean (16)
Kilronan Special School

Winter

Winter is coming around the corner.
The snow will soon be here.
The frost will make the road slippery.
The days are dark and very cold,
The nights are longer too.
I need to wear nice, warm clothes to help keep me warm.

Lisa Stockman (11)
Kilronan Special School

Football

Some kits are ugly
Some kits are nice
But the really bad thing
Is the price.

Some stadiums are very small
Some stadiums are very large
But when it comes to money
They know how to charge.

Some tackles come flying in
Some injuries happen too
And when you're playing football
Make sure it doesn't happen to you.

Some competitions are large
Some competitions are small
It doesn't matter what you're in
You will try to win them all.

Scottish league won by Rangers
English won by Man United
Spanish won by Real Madrid
No matter what happens
We will be very excited.

William Overend (13)
Magherafelt High School

Who Wants To Be A Millionaire . . . ?

Who wants to be a millionaire?
They're just so posh,
So confident thinking they know it all,
And they enjoy showing off,
Arrogant pigs, if they could see themselves.

Who wants to be a millionaire?
They do have good imaginations,
Always thinking of ways to make money,
But they always have to be better than others,
They're so competitive.

Who wants to be a millionaire?
They are loaded,
With all their designer clothes,
Their big, fancy cars,
And they even have private chauffeurs - lazy slobs.

Who wants to be a millionaire?
With their big mansions,
And indoor swimming pools,
Just think of all that fancy food,
And your very own butler to serve it.

Who wants to be a millionaire?
They may be unbelievably rich,
But they will never find true happiness in money,
It changes their personality,
And most of them aren't very nice people.

Do you want to be a millionaire?
I know I don't want to be such a snob.

Stewart Miller (14)
Magherafelt High School

Holidays!

Summer holidays are great,
Getting off school,
Messing about with your friends,
But going on holidays is even better!

Going fast up the runway,
Taking off, making your tummy go funny,
Ears popping, people barfing,
Landing is the next stage.

Stepping out of the aeroplane,
The scorching sun hits your back,
It's sooo hot, especially as I'm wearing jeans and a jumper,
Where we come from it's cold,
Finally we're here - can't wait to see the hotel.

The hotel is lovely, the pool is even better,
We dive into the 3m end, it is soo much fun.
My cousins and I sing in karaoke,
Hey, what do you know, we won! Two in a row.

We go to the beach
And a theme park too.
I go on the two looper,
Come off a looper too!

It's not fair, it's time to go home,
Can't wait to go on holidays
Next year again.

Laura McKeown (13)
Magherafelt High School

The Jungle

In the murky, damp undergrowth
A magical city I saw,
With monkeys, pumas and antelopes
And with their own animal law.

The monkeys were up the trees
Swinging by their long tails.
The humble tortoise tumbling along
No faster than a snail.

The jungle is the most magnificent place
All covered in all shades of green.
The trees are tall and small,
Can you just imagine the scene?

The pools of water
Smile with glee.
The waterfall thrashing against rocks,
You surely must definitely see.

The weather is hot and sticky
And mostly very wet.
I wish I could stay here every day
Because my heart here is surely set.

Neil Burns (13)
Magherafelt High School

Peace Throughout The World!

What's the world coming to?
As nations tear it to shreds.

People so full of spite
Skin colour, beliefs
Who's wrong?
Who's right?
So war is the answer
So countries fight.

People suffering!
It's always the same
So much violence
Too much pain
Do we have to let tears fall again?

People killing and dying
Blood running in rivers
As the hatred of men rages again.

War, it can't make amends
That's what our world's come to
But please can't we change?
Show love to our enemies
Make them our friends!

Lynsey Brown (13)
Magherafelt High School

My Version Of The Animal Alphabet

A is for alligator a deadly animal
B is for buffalo, bees, butterflies and bats
C is for cats both big and small
D is for deer, dogs and dolphins
E is for emu and big, powerful elephants
F is for slippery frogs and small little fish

G as in a greedy goat or giraffe
H as in a horse, a hare or hen
I as in a insect, how they make me shake
J as in a jaguar, no I don't mean the car
K as in a kangaroo or a furry koala bear
L as in a lion, king of all the cats

M, how I want a mouse or a wild mustang
N, how I want a newt, the little slimy customer
O, how I want an ox or maybe an orang-utan
P, how I want a penguin or a parrot
Q, how I want a quail, so small and cute
R, how I want a rabbit or maybe just a rooster

S, I wouldn't mind a snake
T, I would however like a tiger
U is for unicorn, hey wait a minute, they're not real
V is for a tiny vole
W, I wouldn't like a stinging wasp
Z, I would love a zebra.

Victoria Cross (13)
Magherafelt High School

Remember

Remember what it was like being a child again?
Everything excited you
Like birthdays, Christmas, Easter, every little thing.

Remember starting primary school?
New surroundings, new faces, everything different
Teachers were fine, made you feel welcome
Though soon lessons began, a time everyone loved!
When the first day was over you were itching to get back.

Remember being in P7, your last year at primary?
The main thought was the 11+
All the practise tests and revision
Everyone was glad when November came, exams over!

Remember starting high school?
Children looking worried, not knowing anyone
Form class is where everyone starts to talk
The room is now filled with laughter
The bell then rings and we're trying to find our way around
The day is now over
What a day!

I'll look back some day and remember all this,
And smile.

Lauren Lennox (14)
Magherafelt High School

Fireman

Fireman, fireman, how do you do?
Fireman, fireman, how about you?
Fireman, fireman, put out that fire,
'Cause some man longs for that desperate desire.

Fireman, fireman, you saved my life,
Fireman, fireman, you saved my wife.
Fireman, fireman, what can I do?
Just be as brave as you.

Fireman, fireman, you are so brave,
Fireman, fireman, what do you crave?
Fireman, fireman, what do I do?
I want to be just like you.

Fireman, fireman, I am turning insane,
Fireman, fireman, put out that flame.
Fireman, fireman, what can I do?
Ring *999* and they will help you.

Arran Fleming (13)
Magherafelt High School

Netball

The whistle blows and off we go,
Taking shots, and trying to throw,
Trying to mark to dodge for the ball,
As we play we hope we don't fall.

Goals are scored, matches won,
That is why netball is such fun.
Toss-ups, catching, jumping and running,
We all look very cunning.

Foot faults and double bounces are all wrong,
And when we do these our faces look forlorn,
Our coach screams, 'Catch!'
That's what you do at a netball match!

Rebecca Scott (13)
Magherafelt High School

Birthdays!

Your first birthday,
The most important,
Mum will hire a funny clown
So you'll not cry and let her down.

Bouncy castles till you're nine
Money and sweets, having so much fun
Then your friends when they're late
You start to cry 'cause they got the wrong date.

Then you get too old for cake
And Mum doesn't know what to bake
You tell her you're doing it teenage style
Of party hats, there won't be a pile.

Then it comes to your big 40
Mad family and crazy friends, oh no!
Getting older every minute
Then it all comes to a limit.

Presents become less and less
And inside cards it says 'God bless'
No more singing happy birthday
No clowns, no sweets, just fun.

Danielle McIlhatton (13)
Magherafelt High School

My Guitar

My guitar is made of wood and metal.
My guitar is red with a white cover.
My guitar has gold, silver and bronze strings.
My guitar makes your fingers sore.
My guitar has lots of frets galore.
But the most important thing is that my guitar is mine.

John Spallen (12)
Magherafelt High School

Gone

In the big house across the way,
Lived my friend Rebecca - until today.
Six men this morning in a van
Came after breakfast and began
To pack up all the beds and chairs,
The nice red carpet off the stairs,
And all the things I used to see,
When Rebecca invited me for tea.

They took the dishes and the plates
And packed them into wooden crates.
They took Rebecca's CDs, clothes and all,
They took the big clock from the hall.
They took the carpets, tied with strings,
Pots and pans and kitchen things.
They took the sofa bed where we played
(And where we slept the night I stayed).

Cupboards, chests and kitchen stools,
Cooker, fridge and garden tools.
I still don't understand why
They are moving and I let out a sigh.
But now they've gone and shut the door,
And I can't call there anymore.
It's sad to think that from today
I'll never go to Rebecca's to play.

But when I look back . . . memories are sweet,
Playing with Rebecca was really a treat.

Jennifer Brown (13)
Magherafelt High School

Celebrities

They can be posh with lots of attention
Can it be fun for them all?
But their lives can be very confidential
Celebrities have it all.

They have expensive clothes
With big personalities
Always have to be noticed
Celebrities have it all.

They may have their own limo
And a private jet
Their big giant mansion
Celebrities have it all.

Lots of fancy cars
Eating at fancy restaurants
And big fancy parties
Celebrities have it all.

Think they're better than others
Popular everywhere they go
But at times they can be rude
Celebrities have it all.

They're always on TV
Think the world revolves around them
So much money, what do they do with it?
Celebrities have it all.

Yes, they are rich with money
Got all their fame and glory
Can they be happy with all this money, fame and glory?
Do celebrities have it all?

Craig Ritchie (13)
Magherafelt High School

Sing For The Moment

So stop today at work or play
Look around, hear the sound
We never think to stand and stare
So stop this once and have a glare
The sun, the moon, the leaves, the trees
The birds, dogs, cats and bees
We never think of all these things
So we should be happy and we should sing
Stop, listen, hear and taste
And look at your unearthly waste
You destroy everything you can for all you are is man
So think while by the hearth
Of this wonderful and beautiful Earth
For you have life, the rarest thing of all
Don't be put down, everyone can fall
So listen, talk, look while you may, tomorrow could be your final day.

Matthew Hagan (13)
Magherafelt High School

Christmas

Christmas, Christmas, it's all a flash
Christmas, Christmas, it's all a dash
Choral singers singing with lights glowing brightly
Children screaming, they've having such fun
Toys and sweets lying around the house
People on sleighs riding round on the snow
Eating your turkey in front of the fire
An angel on top of the Christmas tree
Money on presents, it's gone down the gutter
Santa's deer are away down the road.

Adam McMenemy (12)
Magherafelt High School

A Horse In A Storm

It was cold, very cold,
The trees looked weak and old,
The young one's being bold,
It was cold, very cold.

Then came the rain,
The sky turned black,
I threw back my head,
When I heard the lightning crack.

The trees looked like cruel men brandishing whips,
The bark looked like gnarled faces,
With brown, hard, crackled lips,
In circles the brave chief paces.

The wind did moan,
I was all alone,
Trees no longer look like clowns,
The wind is slowly calming down.

The woods now filled with a silver mist,
The dew on the grass only just kissed,
Shyly through the trees came a doe with her fawn,
In the horizon the first light breaks at dawn.

Cordelia Mulholland (13)
Magherafelt High School

Party

When I went to a party aged just four,
Someone fell off their chair right down onto the floor.
All the other boys and girls began to laugh and shout,
But I did not, I did not laugh a single bit.
Why didn't you laugh or don't you want to tell?
I didn't laugh a single bit because it was I who fell.

Nevin Riddell (12)
Magherafelt High School

Winter

Winter is a time of year
When Christmas comes around,
There're presents and Santa
And little children all excited.

Winter is a time of year
When it is very cold,
And scarves and earmuffs too.

Winter is a time of year
When it gets darker,
And we have to go in earlier,
Mum's light the fire too.

Winter is a time of year
When we get Christmas holidays,
We have snowball fights,
And we make snowmen too.

Winter is a time of year
When it is freezing cold,
Cars sliding all over the ice,
Frost is hard too.

Winter is a time of year
When only the robin is left,
All the other birds have gone
Far away to nest.

Winter is a time of year
When we all snuggle up together,
All beside each other.

Winter can be cosy with your family,
But winter can be cold with Jack Frost too.

Laura Henry (13)
Magherafelt High School

The Knock!

One night I was on my own,
Munching and crunching my popcorn.
I was watching a horror movie,
Then suddenly there was a knock on the door!

I went to see who was there,
But no one was out there,
Except a hooting of an owl.
After I shut the door the phone rang.

Who could it be at this time of the night?
When I answered, no one was there,
All I heard was breathing,
Then the phone went dead.

Then *knock, knock!* The door again,
But this time there was something,
It was wearing a black hat and coat,
But I couldn't see its hands or face,
Because they were clear like water,
Then it shouted 'Boo!'
I slammed the door and screamed.

Then as I walked into the living room,
The clock kept turning to different times.
Then I heard noises out the back,
Suddenly I heard noises like talking in the living room.

It was a ghost going around the living room,
Then once the clock struck 12, it disappeared.
The next day I heard that it was the lost ghost,
He was called this because many years ago
A man used to live in this house, then he died.
Last night was his anniversary,
This time every year he comes looking for his family that he lost!

Johanna Crawford (12)
Magherafelt High School

Hallowe'en

Hallowe'en, Hallowe'en,
Stick your head in a jelly bean.
Kids come out to trick or treat,
And sometimes say, 'Smell my feet.'
Witches and vampires come out tonight,
When the stars are really bright.
Out will come zombies and bats,
When the dog is asleep on the mat.
See the bright colours of the bonfire,
People stand around and admire.
There is a ring in an apple pie,
If you find it, do not lie.
People are dressing up to give you a fright,
If I was young I'd stay out of sight.
If the children knock on the door, give them some sweets,
If you have none, give them some treats.
Fireworks are to be heard,
Cats and dogs are scared.
Hallowe'en comes just once a year,
So please overcome your fear.

Russell Fullerton (12)
Magherafelt High School

Christmas

C arols sung at Christmas
H appy children play with new things
R olling up big balls to make snowmen
I n the fluffy white snow
S inging jingle bells while we play
T urkey dinner is almost ready
M ore fun for a little while longer
A dults sit inside drinking tea
S inging a song for Christmas time.

Rachel Anderson (12)
Magherafelt High School

Hallowe'en

I always thought Hallowe'en was good
And always seems to have plenty of food
I usually use sweets as treats
But it never seems to work.

Hallowe'en always seems to be funny
But never seems to be sunny
And somehow there is always
Plenty of sweet honey.

Everyone is running around
And playing tricks because they think it's funny
Even throwing the yokes of eggs
Because they think it's a joke.

Well Hallowe'en might be nice
Because everyone is eating plenty of rice
But be careful though
Halowe'en can be *dangerous* . . .

Jonathan Houston (12)
Magherafelt High School

Sleepy Morning

I wake up in the morning,
Another school day to go,
I get dressed in my uniform,
And brush my hair just so.

I go down for my breakfast,
I fancy cheese and bread,
I look round for my mum,
But just see my cats instead.

I shout up to my mum,
'You've slept in, it's after eight,'
She tells me I'm the sleepy head
I'm off school - it's mid-term break.

Richard Hamilton (12)
Magherafelt High School

A Poem About Dogs

My dog is so small,
So golden,
So cute,
He is the best dog ever.

My dog is so big,
So black,
So playful,
He is the best dog ever.

My dog has big, soppy eyes,
So happy,
So glad,
He is the best dog ever.

My dog is so adorable,
So colourful,
So cuddly,
He definitely is the best dog *ever!*

Daniel Kelso (11)
Magherafelt High School

Basketball

Lining up on the court
Running with the ball
Losing by a basket
Other team gets the ball
And they score a basket
One minute to go
The score is all tied
We get the ball
Run towards the net
And score a three pointer
And now, we lift the cup!

Aaron Campbell (12)
Magherafelt High School

Summer

Summer is a favourite time of year,
Which children like to see appear.
No more homework, no more school,
With loads of time to play in the pool.
The sun arrives and out come the flowers,
Down in our meadows the grass does tower.
Along comes a farmer with his mowing machine,
Cutting down the grass, ever so green.
To feed his cows on a cold winter's night,
He is now entitled to take the first flight.
With not a worry of cows or hay,
To relax in the sun so far away.
For now we're are going off to Spain,
Where we are all hoping to see no rain!

Jaime Morrow (12)
Magherafelt High School

The Weather

'What's the weather today?' people say.
The weather, the weather, the weather,
Rain, mist, cloud and sun,
All types of weather to have some fun.
Not just rain to help plants grow,
But frost and the snow for us to throw.
Sun to enjoy with its warm rays of light,
Clouds and wind to make our cheeks go red.
On dark winter nights when it's time to go to bed,
We think,
What will the weather be like tomorrow?
But the sun just winks.

Rebecca Sloan (12)
Magherafelt High School

Hallowe'en

When I think of Hallowe'en,
I think of bonfires burning bright,
And many sparkling colours gleaming,
As the fireworks glow in the sky at night.

When I think of Hallowe'en,
Storytelling of witches and ghosts,
False faces, oh! that look so mean,
And scary letters sent through the post.

When I think of Hallowe'en,
Hot apple pies made for a treat,
With hidden coins for us to find,
Having parties, where the families meet.

When I think of Hallowe'en,
Children playing trick or treat,
Wrapping doors and being mean,
To all the neighbours on the street.

Party costumes of vampires and devils,
Scary nights and lots of screams,
Drinks and fruit and nuts are several,
That's when I think of Hallowe'en.

Ryan Love (12)
Magherafelt High School

Hallowe'en

The children go trick or treating and get lots and lots of sweets
 on Hallowe'en,
Fireworks bang, fireworks crack, but in the end they make a smack.

Toffee apples are so sweet, a scrunchy, tasty little treat.
Pumpkins are scary, so just be wary of what goes on that night.

Streamers flutter all around and make a mysterious sound,
People say costumes are not so scary, but wait until someone
 sneaks up on them!

Jonathan Hurl (11)
Magherafelt High School

Hands Of Time

They are round, square, rectangular of face
Can be hung upon a wall, or set upon a mantelpiece
For hands circle around all day
From seconds to minutes, hours slip away
But in our young life time seems to go slow
Mum often tells me it gets quicker before you know
When everything is going well and we're all having fun
Time slips past, and we think that we have just begun
But in sad and lonely times, the hands seem to stand still
The hours we wish go against our will.

So the golden rule is to enjoy life
No matter how great your troubles or strife
For time will not stop for no man or child
It's just a thought from the clock sitting up *high*.

Vicki McAllen (12)
Magherafelt High School

Clothes Mad!

Clothes, clothes all around
They are always so much more than over a pound

Next, Tammy, New Look too
There I always get something new

Oh so many shops
I think I'm going to drop

Spend, spend, that's always me
Seeing so much on my shopping spree

I love shops
From trousers to tops

Without shops I would be lost
I don't care how much it's going to cost!

Claire Craig (12)
Magherafelt High School

Happy Hallowe'en

H aunted houses stand alone,
A nd ghosts come out of the phone.
P umpkins stand on our doorsteps,
P eanuts in great depths.
Y apping werewolves come out in a full moon.

H orror movies being watched all night long,
A nd zombies come out to sing their song.
L ong, slow, painful deaths,
L ethal scary stories frighten you.
O paque fireworks go off every minute.
W itches fly their brooms overhead,
E xceedingly bloodthirsty vampires hunt for victims,
E xpose frightful skeletons in graveyards,
N ot a good night to go out.

Mark McClenaghan (12)
Magherafelt High School

Happy Days, School's Out

My heart rejoices and I'm thankful too
That school is out for a week or two
No more rushing or pushing in queues
And carrying that heavy school bag was a task to do!
The morning is the worst when my mum shouts
'It's a quarter past eight, you should be out!'
I pull the blanket over my head
And wish I could stay in bed instead
But with weary eyes and tired feet
I shuffle to the breakfast seat
Then I hear, 'It's time to go.'
All I can think of is, *oh no!*

Melvin Fulton (12)
Magherafelt High School

Christmas

Christmas is a time of year,
That brings a lot of Christmas cheer.

On the tree the lights will shine,
And in the rooms we'll smell scented pine.

The parents around the house have to creep,
As all the children are in their beds asleep.

Under the tree the presents are placed,
As the angel from the tree looks down full of grace.

In the morn we will hear the children shout,
And in the distance the church bells are ringing out,

To tell us Jesus was born on this day,
To be thankful for all our gifts we must pray.

Catherine Dempsey (11)
Magherafelt High School

Christmas

In the winter it begins to snow,
Christmas is coming soon we know.
Robins begin to sing too,
It's the most exciting event the whole year through.

It's Santa Claus that little children like,
They hope he'll bring them a new bike.
With tinsel we decorate the Christmas tree,
Lots of presents we like to see.

People like to eat turkey,
And meet up with their family.
Jesus was born on that special day,
He lay in a bed of hay.

Alyson Speer (11)
Magherafelt High School

Christmas

It won't be long till Christmas Day
With lots of presents on the way
I wonder what the weather will be like
Or maybe I should wonder, *will I get a bike?*
Neighbours and friends usually call round
I usually hide until I can be found!
I love Christmas, it brings happiness and cheers
But sometimes our daddies drink too many beers
The food on the table looks lovely and tasty
But the children might be far too hasty
The shopkeepers are busy, their days are never dull
With Santa and his elves, their bags are always full
It has been a long day and it's now time for bed
Thank you for my presents, but most of all being fed.

Vanessa Hawthorne (11)
Magherafelt High School

Green

Green is the grass
Green are the trees
Green are the plants
Which grow in many leaves

Green are some books
Green are some apples
Green are the vegetables
Which we sometimes sample

Caterpillars are green
Frogs are green
Hedges are green
All these things are green.

Megan McKee (11)
Magherafelt High School

Magherafelt High School

M onday morning came
A t last
G rinning I left
H ome
E veryone in first year waited
R acing hearts
A nxious smiles
F unny comments
E ager looks
L aughter
T ension

H igh school life for me - a first year
I 'm very glad to say is
G oing very nicely with
H omework and good days

S chooldays are the best times
C ountless people say
H appily, I find that's true
O ngoing
O pportunity
L ots of things to do.

Richard Brown (12)
Magherafelt High School

The Pet I Want

Maybe I should get a dog
Or a green and slimy frog
Maybe I should get a cat
Or a grey and furry rat
I think I'll get a fish
But it just swims in its dish
I know, I'll get a horse!

Keipher Booth (11)
Magherafelt High School

Seasons

Spring is a time of birth
A time for trees to get new leaves
A time for newborn lambs to run, skip and jump about
And a time to eat berries and mushrooms.

Summer is a time for the beach
To build sandcastles and eat ice cream
Playing sport is really fun
Especially when it's really warm.

Autumn is when the trees
Start to lose their leaves
And as you start to pile them up
You just can't wait to jump into them.

Winter is really cold and frosty
And when snow falls you can have snowball fights
But when the snow melts there's no more fun
But then spring comes and there's joy again.

Andrew Simpson (11)
Magherafelt High School

The Witch

On Hallowe'en night the moon shone bright
For the boys and girls to have a good night.
With crackers and bangers and all the rest,
They enjoyed themselves to the very best.

Over the bonfire flew the old black witch
With her hat and cloak as black as pitch.
And on her broomstick sat a cat,
And it was black and very fat.

The night grew late, the moon went down,
There wasn't a sound about the town.
And everybody was safely sleeping
Except the old black witch who from the clouds was peeping.

Catherine Young (11)
Magherafelt High School

Summer

We are going on holiday to America next week
Which has a very large mountain peak.
There is also a large theme park
Where one of the rides is an ark.

We're going to a beach today
Which is very big.
We will also have to dig
A great big sandcastle.

When I think of the sun
I always think of fun.
Every summer I like to go to the bakery
To get a lovely cream bun.

I always love the months of summer
And I like the way the bees hum there.
As the bees work at the flowers
They have awesome powers.

Elaine Wilson (11)
Magherafelt High School

Holidays With A Yappy Wean!

All the excitement on the plane
I was stuck beside a yappy wean,
When the plane had landed I'd had enough
To see him again would be too tough.

At the hotel I couldn't believe my luck
He was in my pool with a rubber duck,
When I saw him, it made me feel sick
Everyday he would get on my wick.

I went to a theme park, it was my dream
Then I heard a familiar scream,
I looked above the roller coaster train
And there was the yappy wean again!

Bryan Nelson (11)
Magherafelt High School

Winter

Icicles hang
from rooftops.
The snow
never stops.
Snowmen
pop up here
and there
with grass
for hair.
Children have
snowball fights
which last
until night.
Santa Claus
comes out
at night
but when
we wake
he's out of sight!

Kyle Austin (11)
Magherafelt High School

The World

What is in the world today
Apart from money for bills we have to pay?
There is terrorism and war all going on
All through the day long
Many countries, many towns
Some people really are a bunch of clowns!

From September 11th to war between America and Iraq
Many people died and some never came back
So this is what is in our world
Stop and take a look.

Samantha Hagan (11)
Magherafelt High School

What A Fool I Am

You get on your bike
And start to feel free,
You feel like you just got out of jail
Like a feeling you never had.
Then you speed up
Because there's nothing in front of you.
Again you speed up,
You're in a world of your own
Like nothing is going to bother you.
Then suddenly it's over
Like you're all barred up again
Like you have just been stabbed in the back.
Then you have to finally wake up
And say to yourself,
'What a fool I am.'

Nathan Morrow (11)
Magherafelt High School

The Woods

In the woods through the day,
I like to play camps and eat lots of buns
which is great fun.
We have hideouts and caves
with tables, a cupboard for food
and a box of ice for drinks.
We have trees to climb
a stream to dam
and a lake to swim in.
At night rats, cats and bats
come out to play,
with the howling laughter of the wind
and crackling leaves as the fox and badger tread by.

Glenn Henry (11)
Magherafelt High School

Summer

When school is over
Summertime is here.
I can't wait to see
What the weather is going to be.

Going to be beach,
Playing in the sea.
Making sandcastles,
What fun it is going to be.

Going away on holidays,
To somewhere nice and hot.
Staying up late
And not getting up.

When summertime is over
And school is getting near,
I look forward to getting
My new school gear.

Jamie-Lee Harris (11)
Magherafelt High School

My Poem

I've got two dogs called Holly and Jade,
They always seem to misbehave.
Holly is golden, Jade is black,
And with their tail they give you a whack.

They like to play around with a ball,
But they trip you up and make you fall.
They bark all day and through the night,
When they get something in their sight.

I wash them both in dog shampoo,
For they sometimes smell of the loo.
In the mud they like to dig,
And mess around with leaves and twigs!

Annie Stewart (11)
Magherafelt High School

A Special Little Boy

I know a boy, but I can't say who,
He looks lovely dressed in blue.
Dressed in beige or even in green,
He's the prettiest I've ever seen.

This little boy I speak about,
Loves to jump and play and shout.
His days are full of fun and glee,
Who can this little person be?

Although he isn't very old,
He's very clever I am told.
His hair so blond, his smile so sweet,
This little boy you'd love to meet.

Is it Jack or is it John?
It's none of these,
So just guess on.

Gillian Brooks (11)
Magherafelt High School

Passing Cars

Passing cars on the road,
The noise as they drive by,
Far away then close.
Rain pouring, wheels spinning,
The cars slowly approaching,
Then drive away.
When will you come home?
The cars speak their own language,
For those who bother listening.
Awake I hear,
A sign of safe and home,
I can't do anything while you're away,
So I listen to the cars go by,
Waiting until you come home.

Ian Montgomery (13)
Magherafelt High School

My Hair!

Not another bad hair day,
They never seem to go away,
Sticking out here and sticking out there,
It gets me in a fluster, 'Oh my hair!'

Long or short,
Straight or curly,
I always seem to worry, worry,
Will I put it up or keep it down?
Doesn't matter what I do, the look makes me frown.

Brown is so boring,
Should I change to,
Blonde or black or even red?
I want something that will turn heads.

I look in the mirror,
Oh what a sight,
Sometimes it gives me a big fright.

But then again I look around,
And maybe I should just stay brown!

Katrina Steele (12)
Magherafelt High School

My Rabbit

Bouncer is my bunny's name,
White and fluffy like a mane,
Bouncing is his favourite game,
He really is very tame.

I kiss him, I hug him, I hold him tight,
He kicks his feet and thuds in the night,
A carrot in the morning
Makes his eyes glow bright,
A cuddle in the evening fills him with delight.

Laura Davidson (12)
Magherafelt High School

Winter

When winter comes the fields are bare,
The crops have been gathered in with care,
The cattle and sheep are now in their shed
With silage to eat and straw for their bed.

The holly bushes are full of berries so red,
That's how a lot of birds are fed,
Sometimes a robin will come near the door
Looking to find if there's any more.

The days are so short and the nights are so long
And yet the wee birds sing their sweet song,
And snow sometimes comes and the Earth then is white,
It's a beautiful picture - a lovely sight.

The shops, they are stocked up with Christmas fare,
The customers all are very aware,
That it's push and shove for the weeks ahead
And they do their shopping in fear and dread.

It's Christmas morning, the church bell's ringing,
There's a knock on the door, it's carol singing,
Welcome to Jesus born on this day,
Hooray for winter and Christmas Day.

Stephanie Sloss (12)
Magherafelt High School

Cats

Cats like the heat
But they hate the water.
They roll in the peat
And turn black like a potter.

They like to play
And they like to sleep
In a deep bed of hay
Where they don't make a peep.

Jermaine Elder (13)
Magherafelt High School

The School Bully

Who are these pupils?
What's their game?
Why do they taunt us and call us names?

They make life a misery
And school work a bore,
Your work starts to fail as they bully you more.

You'd think they would tire
Of calling names,
The bitchiness and jealousy takes over their game.

But deep down inside
Where no one can see,
Bullies thrive on their actions, 'This is the true me.'

If only they knew
Who they really are,
Wicked and nasty, insecure by far.

It's time to stand up to the bully
And let them see the bullies are the wasters
Not you and me!

Michaela Smyth (13)
Magherafelt High School

Cars

Cars are cool, cars are fast,
Zooming down the road but not too fast.
Wind in my hair, music in my ears,
Foot on the pedal with no fear.

Tearing down the road
Like in Formula One.
Till I reach my destination
I think the race is won.

James Johnston (13)
Magherafelt High School

Hairdresser's Menu

Shiny hair, stylish hair
Which stands out from a mile,
From when you were a baby
Or when you're walking down the aisle.

Glossy hair, coloured hair
Hanging from the root,
Hair that's really short
Or right down to your foot!

Plaited hair, straightened hair,
It's really hard to know,
If you should get a haircut
Or continue to let it grow.

Dry hair, damaged hair,
What are you going to do?
The choice is really easy,
Just try the right shampoo!

It's times like these, when your head goes round
And it's really hard to bear!
So to save all the fuss
You should stick with your natural hair.

Anna Shiels (13)
Magherafelt High School

The Sun

Where the sea looks ever so light
There the sun is shining bright.
Up the road and down the hill
That's where I travel with my friend Bill.

In the morning the sun is shining
You feel alive when you are dining.
In the evening as the sun is setting
For another day it leaves you fretting.

Emma Hogg (13)
Magherafelt High School

Ginger

I am eight inches high,
My tail is curled inwards.

I sleep most of the day,
But when I am awake
I eat and play
And go to the toilet.

The colour of my coat is ginger,
My eyes are green,
My paws are white
And ears are pointed.

My favourite food is Kit-e-Kat,
My favourite toys are furry animals,
My favourite place is on my owner's knee
Or playing in the garden.

In the garden I play
With live animals,
I chase butterflies, but never catch them,
I go after birds but they always fly away
Because of this thing around my neck.

This thing around my neck
It drove me mad at first,
It is blue and orange,
I have worked it out, it's a collar with
A bell that goes ding-a-ling.

Dawn McMullan (12)
Magherafelt High School

The Seasons

In winter when everything is bare,
I look around at the trees and stare.
It won't be long until I know
That leaves and flowers will start to show.
The little birds high up in the tree
Are searching for nuts like a shopping spree.

Now that spring at last has arrived
And everything looks so alive.
The little shoots above the ground
And the birds a place to nest have found.
The little lambs round their sheep,
The small birds cheep and peep.

Ah summer, such a lovely time,
The days are long and the sun will shine.
The farmers are busy in the field,
Their crops to attend so they will yield.
The butterflies in the garden are lovely and bright
And we play 'til late at night.

Now that autumn has come around
The leaves are falling to the ground.
They're red and brown and crunch like crisps
And in the morning we have early mist.
In the fields the tractors drone
As the people sing the harvest's home.

Ross Nicholl (12)
Magherafelt High School

I Love Football

Football, football, football
Is what I love to play.
Running up and down the pitch
Almost every day.

I play football when I'm home
And I play it when I'm out,
I love the sport so much
That I'm never in any doubt.

When I go to sleep at night
I dream about my moves,
So that I can practise them each day
Until I'm in the groove.

When I'm playing in a match
People may place bets,
That when I get the ball
I'll stick it in the net.

Nigel Speer (13)
Magherafelt High School

Honey

Honey - a pot of liquid gold?
No!
My bounding, barking, bouncing,
Friend.
Shimmering, shaking, silky,
Golden.
Pouring herself over me.
Now,
Forever still,
Under
A mound of earth in a shady glen.
At peace
In a golden heaven.

Jill Henderson (12)
Magherafelt High School

The Seasons

Spring is the first to come,
There are new things all around,
Lambs, kittens and plants
And the blossom is on the cherry trees.

Summer is next in line,
It gets warmer and more colourful,
With the flowers all blooming
And all the people are buying them.

Autumn is even more colourful,
Autumn crocuses are out as well as the roses,
With leaves turning golden and red,
Conkers, which children play with, are only one of the other
Seeds scattering across the fields.

Winter is next to come
With the cold rain and wind,
If it snows the world is all white,
Everyone has a fire on and waiting for Santa Claus coming.

This all comes around every year.

Christine Hurl (12)
Magherafelt High School

American Football

American football is for the tough,
That's because it's very rough.
Three teams make the batch,
Only one plays the match.
Offence, defence and the kickers are the batch,
Different skills but they'll win you the match.
Huddle in and make a play,
That's the way to get more pay.
Down on the ground or up in the air,
That's the way to get more ground.
Once you're near your goal
Run it in and go for the score.

Craig Moore (13)
Magherafelt High School

My Family

My dad's the boss,
Well so he thinks,
He's fun and lively
And always up for a laugh.

My mum's on a diet,
It's working quite well,
Not being able to eat
Makes her life hell.

My sisters all three
Are so different from me,
They can't be bothered
With me you see.

Of course there's me
Last but not least,
Youngest and smallest
In the family!

Rachel Taylor (12)
Magherafelt High School

School

School is great
And so fab,
You have 45 periods
In only a week.

When you're at school
You have to behave
With teachers so cross
You might get school rules.

The best things in school
Are maths, English, science and PSE.
There are great teachers
When you do all of these.

Andrew Henry (13)
Magherafelt High School

Love

Love is like
the biggest heart,
with a smile
it is smart.

So if you play
your part,
love will shoot
like a dart.

When you look
in his eyes,
my oh my
time just flies.

And when you
hold his hand,
your mind and heart
is like a band.

When you sing
it makes him feel
like the king
of the world.

Nadine Redpath (12)
Magherafelt High School

My Little Blue Car

My granny had a little blue car
Which used to take her near and far.
She travelled from Antrim to County Down
And couldn't believe her MOT proved unsound.

With sadness and a broken heart
My granny and her car had to part.
Disappointing for her but delight for me
I now race around the fields with glee!

Andrew McClelland (13)
Magherafelt High School

Farming

Farming is always a year round job,
There is always work to do.

Spring

This is when the lambing begins
And the first cut of silage comes in.

Planted are the potatoes and wheat
For all the people to eat.

The cows go out to the field
When the rain has started to yield.

Summer

The second crop of silage is stored away
And when it's sunny, so does the hay.

The sheep and cows graze all day
But the cows will be coming in as autumn's on its way.

Autumn

The wheat is cut
And the potatoes are picked.

The cows are put in the shed
And they are always looking fed.

Winter

Everything is stored away
As winter is here to stay.

Philip Dickson (13)
Magherafelt High School

Water

Water can drip,
Water can run,
Water can freeze,
Water can make you slip.

Water can foam,
Water can change,
Water can hurt,
Water can moan.

Water can,
Water can spill,
Water can kill,
Water can.

Water makes no sound,
Water can be held in something that's round,
Water can rip,
Water can drip.

Water is strong,
Water is gentle,
Water can wave,
Water can be ice.

Water can come as rain,
Water can squirt,
Water can hurt,
Water can go down a drain.

Graham Kirkpatrick (12)
Magherafelt High School

Fairies

Hush don't tell,
There's a secret you must keep.
Down at the bottom of the garden
Is something you would love to meet.

Tread very carefully,
Beware where you stand.
A very delicate creature
Is just about to land.

Her wings are like silver cobwebs
Glistening in the sun.
Everything about her
Is perfectly done.

She carries in her hand
A sparkling silver stick.
And on her back a pouch
That will always do the trick.

It's full of magic dust
To make your dreams come true.
And every single morning
Your day starts anew.

Chloe Anderson (12)
Magherafelt High School

My Motorbike

I like to ride by motorbike
Around the sharp corners and get a fright.
In the wet I might go spinning
But all I think of is winning.
Sometimes I do stunts
Which end up causing bumps.

Jason Scott (12)
Magherafelt High School

Evolution

I think evolution
Is totally not true,
I know that there's a God up there
Who made me and you!

They call it the *big bang!*
When a particle blew up,
That is where we came from,
I think they're all wired up!

Just take a look around you,
Does that not make you think,
That the sunset in the evening
Was made in just a blink?

The raindrops on the window
That once came from the sky.
The big, tall trees around you,
Ant, beetle and butterfly.

Everything was made by God,
Why can't you see
That there is a creator
Who made you and me?

Ruth Scott (13)
Magherafelt High School

My Farm

On our farm we have many animals.
I love my cows, which just say moo.
I help to milk both morning and evening.
But the calves are stubborn, moody and hard to feed.
I hate the pigs, the way they squeal and snap,
But most of all I hate their smell.
I love my hens that lay an egg each day
And best of all I love my collie dogs.

David Allen (12)
Magherafelt High School

Clothes

Clothes, clothes everywhere,
In my wardrobe and in my drawers,
Clothes, clothes in the shops, everywhere you look!

Different styles of clothes,
Granny or old people clothes,
They are as flowery as can be,
Sometimes I wonder where do they get them from?
And then we come to teenage clothes,
The best, the most fantastic clothes on this planet,
I think so anyway,
Wide leg bottoms and chains hanging off trousers
And T-shirts Ma and Da never stop saying,
'Get them things off you, you look horrible.'

Where can we get all these clothes?
We can get them in places such as . . .
Tammy, New Look, Dunnes and many other shops,
Where grandmas would not think of looking
For their flowery dresses, much too cool for them.

Laura Gilmour (12)
Magherafelt High School

My Dog

Sophie is fun
And she can run.
With a sparkle in her eyes
She often whimpers and cries.
She's such a delight
With her coat soft and white.
She's a girl not a boy,
Sophie's my pride and joy,
Her sister lives in Moneymore
So her ears pop when she comes to the door.
Kizzy is her sister's name,
Together they really look the same.

Carly Murphy (13)
Magherafelt High School

What Is Love?

Love is the greatest blessing in the world
That came from the Lord above,
There is a kind of love that is true and trustworthy
That spreads across the ocean like shooting stars.

Love is a moment in everyone's life
That might go wrong or might go right.
Love spreads like blazing fire,
It's the person you most desire.

Love is the key to where all dreams come true
Like the blue skies falling over you.
Love can be hurtful, understanding and painful
But never dies down when you are happy.

Love is a rainbow that sings in harmony
With your heart that sings the everlasting solo.
It will always last for evermore
Because it is human nature that will never fall.

Kerry Halsall (13)
Magherafelt High School

Summer

Summer is like a beautiful day at the beach
When children play with their buckets and spades.
People wear only shorts and T-shirts.
Everyone enjoys playing in the sand.
Little girls and boys jump in the sea,
While waves crash around them.
Jellyfish with their see-through bodies,
Lie on the surface of the water reflecting the sunshine.
Families huddle on rugs eating their picnics.
Pet dogs look on, waiting for crumbs.
As the sun starts to fade, a cool breeze begins to blow.
Parents gather up their belongings,
Rub down feet, arms and legs of unwanted sand.
Cars are packed and homeward go.

Claire Evans (13)
Magherafelt High School

Dad

My dad's name is John,
He's not really that bad,
He's very talkative,
Not at all walkative,
But that's my dad.

He drives a lot in his car,
Never arrives home on time,
He doesn't really care
Which mightn't seem very fair,
But that's my dad.

My dad's quite a dude
With his trendy clothes.
He thinks he's quite cool,
He's really an old fool,
But that's my dad.

He might appear mad
With the way that he dresses.
Others think he looks tough,
He's just a big ball of fluff,
But that's my dad.

Olive Houston (14)
Magherafelt High School

Football

Football is a lovely game.
Every team has a different name.
The cheers of the crowd
And the whistle is so loud.
Saturdays without football wouldn't be the same.
The players go through lots of pain playing in the rain,
But when a goal is scored the crowd go insane.
The scorer runs up the pitch
And they chant his name,
Hoping he will do it again.

Adam Johnston (12)
Magherafelt High School

Down On Our Farm

I live in the country
Quite close to our farm,
And try to keep all the animals
Free from any harm.

I help my daddy with the milking,
It's quite a messy job,
I have to wear an overall
So I look like Builder Bob.

We have one hundred and fifty cows
And each one has to be fed,
So I use our tractor and diet feeder
Up and down the shed.

When all the feeding has been done
We wash the parlour clean,
The cows go into bed for the night
And their comfort is plain to be seen.

Then we have our supper
Which my granny has prepared,
And Daddy and I are both happy
That the workload has been shared.

Trevor Bates (13)
Magherafelt High School

Autumn

'Come little leaves,' said the wind one day.
'Come o'er the meadows with me and play.
Put on your dresses of red and gold
For the summer is gone and the days are cold.'
Soon as the leaves heard the wind's cold call
Down they came fluttering, one and all,
Over the brown fields they danced and flew,
All singing the sweet songs they knew.

Lee Rutherford (13)
Magherafelt High School

My Dog Tess

My dog Tess is black and white,
She plays all day and sleeps at night.
I love to throw the ball for her,
She won't bring it back, that's for sure!

Tess loves food and eats so much,
I always give her a bit of my lunch.
Her favourite is chocolate milkshake,
But I don't share my yummy cake.

We use Tess to round up sheep,
Hoping she won't make a peep,
Because if she does, the sheep will run,
Then we will have some fun!

When no one's about I bring her inside,
She runs around and tries to hide.
If Mum comes back, we're in trouble,
So we have to get out fast, on the double.

Henry Stewart (12)
Magherafelt High School

Wrestling

The wrestling event starts with excitement.
The fans cheer and boo.
The lights dim and the music starts,
The wrestling superstars enter the ring.

The fight begins with punches and kicks.
The Rock kicks Stonecold.
Stonecold fights back with a body slam
But the Rock hits him with a chair.

Stonecold puts the Rock through a table.
The Rock, rockbottoms Stonecold to the floor
But suddenly he retaliates with a mighty punch,
Leg drops and stunners him 1, 2, 3.

Harry Evans (13)
Magherafelt High School

My Rabbit Floppy

I once had a rabbit
Which was black and white,
He was called Floppy
And he loved to fight.

He always growled
When I cleaned out his bed,
But he loved when I cuddled him
And patted his head.

He once had a brother
Who was nicknamed Thumper,
They played together
Rolling round in a jumper.

Dear Floppy didn't eat
No matter what was bought,
And now that he's gone
I miss him a lot.

Rachel Hilman (13)
Magherafelt High School

School

I wake up every morning dreading
The place where I'll soon be heading.
I pack my bag and then I pray
I haven't forgotten my homework today.

I meet my friends when I arrive
And then I'm happy for a while.
But once I get to class
I soon forget how happy I was.

Every day is just the same, work, work, work . . .
Then homework . . . again!
I wish some day I could just go
To Disneyland, instead of school.

Annette Henderson (13)
Magherafelt High School

My Farm

The bull is roaring and threatening to kill someone who comes close.
The rooster is crowing at 7 o'clock in the morning
when I have to get up.
The hens are squawking with hunger.
The cows are looking for silage and to be milked.
The door of the calf house is creaking as it swings
backwards and forwards.
The cat quietly creeps across the floor of the house.
The dog spots her and runs madly after her barking furiously.
The pigs squeal as they fight over their food and water.
The baby chicks wander around chirping and cheeping.
The sheep say 'baa, baa,' as they wait for their hay.
The tractor is started and ready for ploughing.
The farmer takes position and shoots at the crows.

Brian Forsythe (12)
Magherafelt High School

Hallowe'en!

Look up in the sky,
Watch the fireworks fly by.
You see witches with hats
And tiny black cats.
Children knocking on your door,
They always come back looking for more.
Some children playing tricks
And toffee apples they lick.
As the bonfire flickers in your eyes
And it grows to an enormous size.
At the end of the night
It's time to set things right,
By going to bed
And saying goodnight.

William Pickering (14)
Magherafelt High School

First Day At School

My first day at school is nerve-wracking,
Walking through the front door,
Long corridors, it's scary and exciting,
Not knowing what lies ahead.

No second, third or senior pupils
Looking down on us,
Laughing, teasing, tripping us just for fun,
No one to threaten us or make us feel small.

Filing out of the assembly hall in our little rows.
First class of the year, I wonder how it will go!
Time to move on to the next class already,
Hope I don't forget my way.

Maths, English, science, all nice teachers so far,
Last class, art and it's 3.15pm already.
Time to go home, excitement over.
First day at school, better than I thought.

Helen Hawthorne (11)
Magherafelt High School

Football

Football is so much fun,
It's even better in the sun.
Everybody is put to the test
To see if they will play their best.
And when the game's about to start
I really love it with all my heart.
Some players just can't get to the ball
Even the ones who are pretty tall.
But when they score into the net
Some poor bloke has lost a bet.

Lee Weir (13)
Magherafelt High School

Holidays

Everyone likes to get time off,
Away from school or away from work,
Time to relax and have some fun,
Go out for dinner or perhaps a walk.

Some people like to go to the sun,
Lie on the beach or play in the pool.
Others enjoy to ski in the snow,
Instead of the heat, they prefer the cool.

Holidays come at different times of the year,
Christmas, Easter, summer, Hallowe'en.
Time to meet family and friends
Or visit places we've never seen.

I love all holidays,
Whatever the weather.
Time off school,
I wish they'd last *forever.*

Matthew Stewart (11)
Magherafelt High School

Christmas, Christmas

Christmas, Christmas full of joy
For each and every girl and boy.
Christ was born on Christmas Day
In a lowly cradle, full of hay.

Christmas, Christmas my family gather,
That's the day we talk to our father.
After church we all return home
And I compose a Christmas poem.

Christmas, Christmas the end of the day,
All the visitors have gone away.
It's off to bed for me to stay
Until tomorrow, when it's Boxing Day.

Paul Tang (13)
Magherafelt High School

Football

Football is good,
Football is fun,
Football puts me in a good mood.

Footballers are wealthy,
Footballers are fussy,
Footballers are very healthy.

A yellow card comes before a red,
A yellow card comes from a ref,
A yellow card comes after lazy Ned.

A goal is very important,
A goal is everything a player would want,
A goal is a very happy moment.

Fans go crazy,
Fans go mad,
Fans go celebrating and don't stay lazy.

Celebrating after the match,
Celebrating with other fans,
Celebrating becomes a catch.

William McIlhatton (12)
Magherafelt High School

Summer On The Farm

Farmers are cutting silage and maize,
The cows are grazing in the fields,
Lots of room for them to graze.

The farmers are harvesting the grass
Making hay as the winter feed,
Stacking bales to let the machines go past.

As the nights grow longer
The jobs last longer,
Far less time to sit and ponder.

Richard Patterson (11)
Magherafelt High School

I Hate School

I hate school,
Many children do,
What about you?

I think schools a trap,
All we do is
Work, work, work.
We start at nine
And work till three.

Then home I go
With my school bag full,
More work to do,
Homework of course,
It's all very boring at school.

People say these school days
Are the best days of your life.
Well, I think they're wrong
Because when you're at school
There is no life.

When will I ever be free?

Richard Love (13)
Magherafelt High School

My Dad

My dad is kind,
My dad rides a bike,
My dad drives a tractor sometimes,
My dad is a laugh,
My dad is a good person,
My dad likes a Coke,
My dad likes his food,
My dad likes being himself,
My dad is simply the best.

Mervyn Bowman (11)
Magherafelt High School

Autumn

Autumn time is here again,
It's my favourite time of the year,
Leaves falling, chestnuts dropping
In the cooling gentle breeze.
Frosty nights when I'm tucked up in bed
Thoughts of harvest go through my head,
Farmers busy in the fields,
Storing up for winter's meals.
Animals scurry all around
Looking for food on the ground.
Children's voices sound all around
As they play in the crisp icy air,
Red noses and cheeks, how they glow!
'Look up, do you think it will snow?'

William McClenaghan (11)
Magherafelt High School

Farm Tractors

F arming is fun
A nimals are great
R abbits need looking after often
M ud is everywhere.

T railers are carting silage
R olling grass on top of the pit
A ll tractors need four large wheels
C utting the grass is rather cool
T ipping the load is very slow
O liver tractors are very old
R enaults are much more modern
S everal are needed on any farm.

Alan Hyndman (11)
Magherafelt High School

Animals That I Have

Animals are cute and cuddly,
You can hold them and walk them,
You can train them to be good.

I love hamsters so, so much,
They are very cute and cuddly.
You can play with them every day,
They live in cages with lots of warmth and sawdust.

Puppies are cute and cuddly,
You can walk and play with them,
You have to feed them every day,
You have to put them to bed every night.

Dogs and puppies go bark, bark,
Hamsters go scratch, scratch
When lying in their little beds,
They like to be played with every day.

Jan Arrell (11)
Magherafelt High School

Animals

Sheep, sheep like to eat,
Sheep, sheep have a croaky bleat.
Sheep, sheep have lots of wool,
Sheep, sheep are not very cool.

Dogs, dogs are very kind.
Dogs, dogs so grand and fine.
Dogs, dogs are very warm,
Dogs, dogs have lots of charm.

Pigs, pigs are very smelly,
Pigs, pigs wobble like jelly.
Pigs, pigs are very snorty,
Pigs, pigs aren't very sporty.

Gavin Brown (12)
Magherafelt High School

If I Ruled The Skool . . .

If I ruled the skool . . .
Everyone could sleep in and come in when they want,
Homework would be very brief,
Plenty of breaks for all,
Wear whatever clothes you want,
Lots of refreshments all day long,
Have some pop musicians visit,
What a better way to spend skool.

If I ruled the skool . . .
I'd have parties on Fridays,
The walls would be bright colours of the 80s,
Luxury TVs, and DVDs for every class,
No teachers, lots of fun children all the way,
We would need no headmaster because of course I'd be in charge,
I will run the skool, it would be like 1, 2, 3.

It's Friday and it's party day,
We partied till dawn,
It was great fun,
Now it's over I can't wait till another skool week starts.

Cherith Scott (14)
Magherafelt High School

Swimming

Swimming is my hobby,
I just can't stop going.
Swimming in the big pool
Makes me feel so good.
Swimming with my new school
To the leisure centre I go.
Swimming in a team again,
I wonder will we win?

Julie Morton (11)
Magherafelt High School

Christmas Time

C herry brandy, have a swing
H appy children everywhere
R udolph lands on the roof
I vy over every door
S tockings hang from the fireplace
T ime to go to bed early
M erry Christmas everyone
A nd a happy new year
S anta Claus is coming tonight.

T urkey dinner at 1 o'clock
I n the night we hear a bump
M any presents to be opened
E very night we sit and pray that Santa
  will come another day.

Lesley Jackson (13)
Magherafelt High School

Me

I have blue eyes
And am very shy.

I have small feet
And am very neat.

I am very pale
But I am not frail.

I'm very small
Just like a doll.

I dance and sing
To anything.

This is me
And I am free.

Melissa Irvine (11)
Magherafelt High School

Seasons

In spring the lambs jump freely,
The birds start to nest,
The grass gets greener,
The flowers begin to grow,
The hens lay eggs,
The days get longer
And the farmers sow their seeds.

In summer we get our holidays,
In summer we go on holidays,
The sun shines,
The farmers cut their grass,
All the kids play,
The animals go to market
And the days are longer.

In autumn the leaves change colour,
The leaves also fall,
The farmers bring in the harvest,
Conkers fall from trees,
The days get shorter,
Hallowe'en comes upon us
And it gets colder.

In winter we get snow,
We get more school holidays,
Christmas comes upon us,
We light an open fire,
The days are short,
All the kids play
And then we get new year.

Matthew Gallick (13)
Magherafelt High School

The Months Of The Year

January brings the snow
That makes our feet and fingers glow.
Shivers in the night
Make us lie in bed with fright.

February brings the rain,
That thaws our lakes again,
Out with our raincoats,
And on with our hats again.

March brings breezes loud and chilly
That shake about the daffodillies,
The doors they bang open and shut
That leaves me stuck in a rut.

April brings the spring so sweet
In the garden daisies at our feet,
The grass is as green as ever,
Boy these months are so clever.

May brings out the little lambs,
Skipping beside the dams,
Next we know we're in the field
To help reap the yield.

June brings tulips, carnations and roses,
My mum, her hand full of posies,
In the meadow are horses and cattle,
Running about as if in battle.

July brings heat with cooling showers
To water all the flowers,
The days are now so much longer,
Boy I love the summer.

August brings the fields of corn,
Once again the harvest is born,
Through the fields and in the hay
This is where I like to play.

September brings the fruit
Sportsmen then begin to shoot,
Because this is what you will hear
At this time of year.

October brings the pheasant
To collect the nuts is pleasant,
Hallowe'en is close at hand,
It is now starting to turn so bland.

November brings the wind and blast,
To make the leaves blow really fast
And now in a trice
What was water has turned to ice.

December brings the sleet
But also the Christmas treat,
Every fence and every tree
Is as white as it can be.

Aaron Ferguson (11)
Magherafelt High School

Potatoes

Potatoes, potatoes in the ground,
You have to look so they can be found.
Raining or shine we work away
Till the end of each day.

Now we have a harvester
Things are faster and warmer too,
But to tell the truth I'd rather watch Scooby Doo.

Then comes wintertime,
Ready for the picking and bagging,
It's so cold you definitely need padding.

Then the springtime comes,
Time for planting in the soft ground,
Once the machine goes in the potatoes cannot be found,
Oh to next autumn time it will all begin again.

David Barfoot (14)
Magherafelt High School

Sport

With everybody running about,
Having people say, 'You're out.'
Young and old helping out.
I love going fishing and catching a trout.

Teams have to train
Even in the rain.
In any sport you do your best,
Now you are better than the rest.

Knees are scraped and legs are broken,
Sometimes you get a cup as a token.
People sometimes shout boos
But only when you lose.
Ready, steady go you mustn't lose,
Then it's up to you if you win or lose.

In these games there are many rules,
Sometimes if you don't obey you be treated like a fool.

There are many different types of sport,
Hooray for the other team, he hit it over the bar,
Even for the teams it is sweet and sour.

Be the best you can,
Even if you can't keep calm.
Sometimes if you hit a football fan,
You could end up with a ban.

Trying the best you can,
Hearing team-mates say you can.
I heard this from my fellow man,
Never ever say you can't,
Go do your best and hear your name as a chant.

There is so much you can choose from, volleyball,
Basketball and football, no excuse at all.
Even if you are not that tall,
Really trying your best, that is most important of all.

Paul Johnston (13)
Magherafelt High School

Saturdays

Saturdays are great,
I always have a nice lie-in,
I also ride my quad,
It can go pretty fast
And its skids are really cool!

I always walk my dog,
He chases loads of rabbits,
He can be very naughty
And always has lots of fun,
Then gets his dinner and eats like a pig!

I then go on a cycle,
I cycle up the road
And then cycle back,
Always looking about,
Never knowing what's next.

Then I go to my cousin's,
He has a quad as well,
With this we're out for hours
Until the rain decides to come,
We then know our fun is over!

The best part was still to come,
Feeding the animals on his farm,
This was the highlight of my day,
Seeing the little lambs at play,
They were always full of fun.

Then we go back home
After a lovely gleeful day,
I slump back into my bed,
Watch a film
And surrender to sleep!

Alan Simpson (12)
Magherafelt High School

The Haunted House

There is a haunted house
That stands upon a tall hill,
Surrounded by shadows and darkness
When everything is still.

They say the house is evil,
Mounted upon pure hate,
Dark souls walk the grounds
And re-enact their terrible fate.

Murders have been held there
And screams can still be heard,
But no one will talk about the house
As they are far too scared.

They say if you dare visit
You dig your own grave,
Your life it will be taken
And your spirit will become a tortured slave.

So don't pay a visit
For nothing stirs, not even a mouse,
Don't risk waking the spirits
In the forsaken haunted house.

Emma Campbell (14)
Magherafelt High School

Christmas

Waiting for Christmas is lots of fun
now we have got rid of all the sun.
Out comes the snow
oh, it's winter what do you know.

Waiting up that night,
might give some people a fright.
Waiting anxiously to see what's in store,
afraid to open the living room door.

Waiting full of joy
to see if Santa has left my toys.
We left biscuits as a treat
to see what he could eat.

As time draws near to getting up
I went to see what was in the cup.
Oh look, Santa has drunk all his tea
how much happier could I be?

I slowly opened the living room door
to see what was in store.
My eyes were full of joy
as I plundered through all the wonderful toys.

Karen Evans (13)
Magherafelt High School

Christmas

Christmas brings lots of snow,
Frost lying on the ground,
Children in their warm winter clothes,
Getting off school for Christmas holidays,
Snowmen being built,
Decorating the Christmas tree,
Sending out all the Christmas cards,
Wrapping all the Christmas presents,
Sleighs sliding down the hill,
Children starting snowball fights,
Turkey dinners cooking in the kitchen,
Singing Christmas carols,
Sitting by the fire in the cold winter nights,
Watching all the Christmas films,
Remembering baby Jesus being born,
Ponds freezing over with thick ice,
Going to town for Christmas shopping,
Children waiting for brilliant presents,
Presents waiting to be opened,
People getting ready for Christmas.

Pamela Stewart (14)
Magherafelt High School

Hallowe'en

H is for Hallowe'en when we have lots of fun,
A is for afterwards when we have finished,
L is for love once you meet a girl,
L is for living like we all do,
O is for objects that we hit with fireworks,
W is for water which we put on used fireworks,
E is for evil which some people are on Hallowe'en,
E is for everything that we do on that night,
N is for never hold lit fireworks.

Kenny Bradley (13)
Magherafelt High School

Parents! Who Needs Them?

Yap! Yap! Yap!
That's all they ever do.
Don't do this and don't do that,
You haven't got a clue.
They're constantly shouting and never ending scolding,
Well I'll tell you something, I'm fed up with their mouthing.

Moan! Moan! Moan!
It really gets on my nerves.
Why are parents always cross at us?
Whatever it is we do.
Are we really that cheeky to our parents?
Well I am, sometimes, are you?

Oh, they're not all that bad
Although they can get a little mad,
But that's just mums and dads.
It wouldn't be the same if they were any other way.
I know, they'll come to their senses some day.

Andrea Watters (14)
Magherafelt High School

Brotherly Love Means . . .

Sometimes we say things we don't mean,
Sometimes these things are cold and mean,
But we don't mean these things, we just . . . say them!

These things can hurt all mankind,
I'm sorry for the things I said, not being kind,
I find it hard to say what's really on my mind,
But the way I love you I'll never again find.

Brotherly love fits like a glove, so warm, so tight, like a bear hug,
Brotherly love not something you find,
You just know - it's always there, at the back of your mind.

Adam Kells (11)
Magherafelt High School

My Rabbits

My two little rabbits
Are lovely you see.
My mum and dad bought them
Especially for me.

One of them is black,
The other is brown.
They are so full of mischief
They make me frown.

The names of my rabbits
Are Bugsy and Rob,
But trying to get them to know their names
Was such a job,
But now they know their names it's fine,
They walk after me all the time.

Now they are bigger,
To my surprise,
My black bunny rabbit
Showed me five pairs of baby eyes.

Two babies are white,
One is black,
One is brown
And the other is grey.
Now my baby rabbits are doing well in every way.

We are one big happy family,
My rabbits and me,
Because I love them
And they love me.

Natasha Hillyard (11)
Magherafelt High School

Tigers

Tigers are fast and furious,
Tigers are fluffy,
Tigers are scruffy,
Tigers are huffy,
Tigers are aggressive,
Tigers are fierce,
Tigers are scary,
Tigers are advanced,
Tigers are cute,
Tigers are massive,
Tigers are *big,*
Tigers are small,
Tigers are loud!
Tigers are boring,
Tigers are accurate,
Tigers are bold,
Tigers are white and black,
Tigers are orange and black,
Tigers are good,
Tigers are cool,
Tigers are wired,
Tigers are amazing,
Tigers are bad.

Mark McClelland (11)
Magherafelt High School

Cats

Cats are big,
Cats are small,
Cats are bold,
Cats are smart.

Cats are black,
Cats are orange,
Cats are all different colours,
Cats are nasty,
Cats are nice.

Cats are boring,
Cats are playful,
Cats are ugly,
Cats are beautiful,
Cats are fluffy,
Cats are not fluffy.

Cats have nasty claws,
Cats can hurt you,
Cats are noisy,
Cats are quiet.

Cats are strong,
Cats are weak,
Cats are intelligent,
Cats are silly,
Cats are sensible.

Cats are fat,
Cats are thin,
Cats are smelly,
Cats are full of energy,
Or cats can just lie and sleep all day.

Alanna Johnston (12)
Magherafelt High School

My Pets

I have a pet but what could it be?
It could be a rabbit or a dog
Or even a crocodile or a lion.

It is a really tall animal
With big feet,
He's my best friend.

He has a black muzzle,
With big cheeks
And big, brown eyes.

My pet has
A long tail
And is a brindle colour.

My pet is a pedigree
And goes to shows.
Of course, it's my dog Shadow.

I have another pet, but what could it be?
She likes to run, jump and leap.

I have another pet, but what could it be?
She's really tall and is brown,
Her name is Chestnut.

I have another pet, what could it be?
She's a bit bad because she eats the fence,
But she's my best friend.

I have another pet, but what could it be?
She stays in the paddock and goes to shows,

Of course, it's my horse, Chestnut!

Rachel Henry (12)
Magherafelt High School

Summertime

Summer is the best of times,
Listening to the ice cream chimes,
I love climbing trees,
I hope I don't get chased by bees.

Running about in the sun,
Oh it is good fun,
Splashing and playing in the pool,
Oh it keeps me nice and cool.

Grandad puts the trampoline out,
All my cousins start to shout,
I am jumping so high,
I can nearly touch the sky.

My mummy gets on to have a go,
We all think she is rather slow,
Auntie Caroline jumps up for a turn,
The sun shines down and makes her burn.

We have got our holidays from school,
This is oh so neat and cool,
Nine long weeks we are off,
I hope I don't get a cough.

We are going to the zoo,
There is a giant kangaroo,
This is our summer treat
And it is really very neat.

The evenings are really very fine,
It is nearly time to dine,
Let's get out the barbecue,
Everyone rushes to form a queue.

Summer seems to go so quick,
It seems to be a great big trick,
Now it is time to go,
Oh I hope this summer will go slow.

David McAllen (12)
Magherafelt High School

A Party At Hallowe'en

The party at Hallowe'en
Started with a bang,
My friends all jumped
For joy
To see the fireworks rise.
They hissed and banged,
It really was
A beautiful sight.

In the distance
Sticks crackling,
Tyres burning,
Flames in the air
High as the sky,
Orange, yellow, reds,
Colours glow.

Children dancing,
Playing games,
Oh, what a sight to see,
Games have started,
Dunking for apples,
Playing conkers.

The smell of apple tarts
In the distance,
Food's ready,
Let's all run,
Apple tarts,
Sticky buns,
Monkey nuts,
It really was all fun.

Laura Anderson (11)
Magherafelt High School

My Holiday

My holiday in July was one I'll never forget, with Gran,
for a bit of a crack paddling around with her floppy sun hat.

As my friends and I gathered, my tired, good old dad told me
the tide was getting high. We all slid into our sleek and groovy
wetsuits and soon hit the water.

With a splash and a dash we all clashed into the shimmering water
enjoying the crack of all the others.

As the harbour got crowded we fled up the escape ladder,
and had a good old chatter on the sandy shore.
We met Tom and John and had a good game of shore-gore,
and a few more, it was very good.

With Barry's insight we soon hung up our wetsuits and dried them
with the sunlight, dressed in white, knocked ourselves, in full flight
and enjoying the night with all our might.

Steven Higgins (12)
Magherafelt High School

Drugs!

Ecstasy, cannabis and cocaine
We would have to be mad
Or totally insane!
LSD, speed, even weed,
Stealing or mugging
This expensive habit to keep,
Magic mushrooms, solvents,
Alcohol and fags
Readily available
Non-expensive to buy,
High effects, side effects,
Near fatal then death.
Your choice!
Your call!
Your body!
Your life!

Alixs Ferguson (12)
Magherafelt High School

Weather

Weather can change
At any time.

When there is a sun,
It is warm and bright,
We could have a heatwave,
Which means it's very hot.

The clouds close over,
They get very black,
Then the rain starts
Pouring down,
It would get wet
And usually quite cold.
When the wind starts
The trees blow about,
The wind and the rain
Smash against the rooftops,
The thunder roars and
The lightning strikes.

There is snow on the ground,
Very cold and very white.
The roads are slippery,
Frost everywhere,
Shining bright,
Icicles hanging
From the rooftops.

The fog comes down,
We can't see a thing,
It is now very damp
And also quite misty.

Why is the weather so changeable?

Aaron McLean (11)
Magherafelt High School

The Stormy Day

I woke up in the morning
Hoping to see the sun,
But heard the pelting rain
Beating on the windows.
It was such an awful sight,
Rivers were overflowing,
Hailstones pelting down, I tried to get out of bed
But I couldn't stand the pain,
It was simply just too cold.

I pushed myself out of the bed,
Ran downstairs,
Hoping it was all just a dream,
But sadly it wasn't.
I put on my Wellingtons
To go and feed the rabbit,
But when I opened the door,
Whoosh! All the water came in,
I was so cold,
My teeth were chattering
And my legs were shaking.

I went and looked out the window,
I didn't know what to do.
There was thunder and lightning,
Then suddenly the lights went out.
It started to snow,
I went to bed shivering,
I woke up hoping to see the sun.
No such luck,
Snow and hail were still falling
My teeth were still chattering,
But worst of all,
The *heating pipes had frozen.*
I hate stormy days.

Lauren Scott (11)
Magherafelt High School

The Flower

All alone in the garden
Standing in the wintry wind
Early in the morning
Whispering in the wind
It would be saying, 'Can I be your friend?'
It was dancing in the garden
Desperate for a friend.
It was standing, staring into my eyes,
I was feeling sorry for it,
It was bobbing up and down,
For I was going,
Going to pick it up.
I grabbed it, put it in a jar,
I took it into the kitchen,
My mum came in and said,
'What a lovely flower.'

Colder and colder it got every day,
Mourning, the flower, most of the day,
No longer it danced every day,
The petals on the flower
Were freezing even more.
The petals were brown and crunchy,
No smells of that beautiful flower,
My mum was sad,
It was dying away,
That I sadly have to say,
That lovely little flower that in spring
Looked a lovely little thing.
It had died peacefully,
That lovely little flower.

Samantha Speirs (11)
Magherafelt High School

School

At 9.15 the bell must go
Into form rooms we must go.
Everyone in uniforms
Discreet to be the same
When we start a new day
Of our school life.

At 9.25 our classes start,
Oh no, science first for me.
Everyone hurdling and running about,
Trying not to be late
Or they'll be in trouble.

Yey, it's break time,
Time to chat
But not too long
Running about the huts.

Back into class again
Time for studies to begin,
Lots of science and RE today.

It's lunchtime now.
Oh I'm so hungry I could almost eat a ton,
Only have 30 minutes to spare,
Back to class again.

Back to class again
Only three more periods to go,
Oh English next,
But not that French,
At 3.15 we're out of school.

Diane Booth (11)
Magherafelt High School

Cars

Cars are fast,
Cars are slow,
Cares are petrol,
Cars are diesel,
Cars are small,
Cars are big,
Cars are fat,
Cars are sporty,
Cars are cool.

Cars have tinted windows,
Cars don't have tinted windows,
Cars are loud,
Cars are not loud,
Cars are smelly,
Cars are clean,
Cars are dirty,
Cars are old,
Cars are new.

David Burrows (12)
Magherafelt High School

Me 'N' Me Da

Me 'n' me da,
Are great buddies ye know,
We're both football crazy
When the red shirts of Arsenal
Play on the tele.

A round of golf,
Me 'n' me da play
But I keep the score
'Cause when he's swinging,
I have to shout, 'F . . . O . . . R . . . E!'

When I grow up,
So they all say,
I'll be the spit of me da
That'll be OK!
It won't be so hard,
'Cause everyone knows
He's only five foot five,
So I won't have far to grow!

Nicky Brown (11)
Magherafelt High School

My Dog Bond

My dog Bond
Is big and black,
If he sees a sight of a cat,
He will bark and bark.

He tries to get out
But does not succeed
Because he's only after a great feed.

He tries to play football,
Running hard he does not fall
As he only wants to burst the ball.

When I put him to bed,
He shakes, shakes and shakes his head
Then runs into his comfortable bed.

When I go to close the gate,
Bond goes for a long sleep
And doesn't come out the next day till late.

David Mawhinney (11)
Magherafelt High School

The Aliens

The aliens are coming,
They are coming down to Earth.
They want to suck our brains out,
They want to have a feast.

The UFO is landing,
The lights are shining brightly.
The aliens come down the steps,
They walk towards the crowd.

They have tear-shaped heads
With big, black, beady eyes,
Light green skin stretched tightly
Over their short, thin bodies.

The speak a strange language,
It is very soft and slow.
Everyone is afraid of them,
We hope that they will go.

Leigh Gibson (11)
Magherafelt High School

Driving At Eleven!

Driving at eleven,
amazing that,
it must be fun,
it might even be like Heaven.

So what would it be like to be driving at eleven?
You could go fast, you could go slow,
but I could go anywhere I know.

I could go up hills,
I could go in the snow,
I could go in the rain,
I could go anywhere I know when I'm driving at eleven.

Robin O'Neill (11)
North Coast Integrated College

When

When will it end,
The pain and the tears,
This ruthless cruelty
That I've suffered for years?

When will it end,
This torture, this aching?
My body is alive
But my heart is slowly breaking.

When will it end,
The sadness and crying?
Am I ultimately destined
For a lifetime of sighing?

So when will it end,
This heartache and sorrow?
I live through today,
I pray for tomorrow.

Jaimie White (17)
North Coast Integrated College

Shadow!

It was a stormy night,
The wind was up,
I could see in my sight
A light shining bright.

I saw a shadow in the back
Saw it shine, shine so bright,
The shadow grew black, black, black
Until it slid its body into a hole.

Was it an animal or was it a fly?
For it slid in that hole with a gentle cry,
Will I ever know? Will it come out?
    I will never know!

Linda Stewart (11)
North Coast Integrated College

The Holiday

Bring! Bring! up I get
Step into the shower
Boy, it's hot!
Down to breakfast
Toast and bacon, what's that noise?
It's a fire engine.

Here we are in the car,
Beep! Beep! out of the way!
Park the car and off we go -
We go through the detector,
Beep! Beep! we're gone!

Waiting for the plane,
Here it is.
Wait a minute, they have to put the fuel in.
Boarding now, just can't wait.

Up and away in the air,
Vroom! Vroom! Vroom! land we're flying away!
Bump! Bump! Bump! here we are
But, oh no! my vomit came up!

Here's the bus, in we get
Uh oh! forgot the CD player!
Didn't tell
Got the luggage.
Here we are in Portugal!

Alistair Alan Chambers (12)
North Coast Integrated College

This Season

Man U are going to win this season,
They'll sweep Arsenal off their feet,
Gerard Houllier wants a reason
For Owen's two left feet.

Alex Ferguson has the feeling
They'll win the Champions League,
Christiano Ronaldo with a hat-trick
The crowd will sit and watch the magic.

This time we'll beat Real Madrid,
Beckham will come crawling back,
Ronaldo will get sent off for diving
He'll pretend to hurt his back.

The FA Cup will be taken from Arsenal,
United will win it this time,
We'll beat them five-nil if not more,
It would be the best match of all time.

This time we'll win the Worthington Cup,
Man U and Liverpool in the final,
Of course they'll win every cup they can.
That's what will happen this season.

Justin Kane (11)
North Coast Integrated College

I Like

I like eating cheeseburgers,
I could eat them all day.
I like Man United,
they are my favourite team.
I like Fanta orange,
I wish it was rain.
I would like Old Trafford
and Nou Camp in my backyard.
I would like it if bees
and wasps vanished forever.
I would like to never grow old
and live forever.
I would like it if money grew on trees.
I would like it if you could
do magic all day.

Reuben Hasson (11)
North Coast Integrated College

My Favourite Things

I like the white fluffy snow
And the Easter bunny's white
Fluffy tail.
Christmas is fun!
Christmas is great with all the
Snow and Christmas trees.
I like it when the sun comes out and
Dries up all the snow
And in its place there's a rainbow.
I like to be warm and cosy
And eating chocolate, while
Looking at the green fields.
I like to go on the computer
Then go on the PlayStation 2!

Paul McAlister (11)
North Coast Integrated College

If

If cars could fly,
And grass ate goats,
If we couldn't die,
Then cats could float.

If teachers wore uniforms,
And fairy tales were true,
If boats sailed on the motorway,
Then your teeth are blue.

If birds acted like monkeys,
And animals didn't have hair,
If hearts were yellow,
Then that would be rare.

If maths was really easy,
And you listened to your conscience,
If your brain was working properly,
Then you wouldn't be reading this nonsense.

Charlotte Beckett (12)
North Coast Integrated College

New School

N ew school, great!
E veryone enjoys school.
W ouldn't change to go back to primary school.

S ubjects I haven't done before
C lassrooms much bigger.
H omework's okay
O ther friends you can meet
O nly some things I don't like.
L ots of new teachers!

Natasha McCloskey (11)
North Coast Integrated College

Wolf!

A wolf lives out in the wilderness,
Waiting and waiting for the night to creep up.
Darkness slithers over the land,
The wolf has awoken.

The wolf runs silently,
Like a river running in a valley.
It reaches its destination,
Eyes gleaming, it begins its howling.

The moon is full,
Like a bright light among the stars.
The wolf goes on howling,
Its fur ruffled by the wind.

Slowly the wolf creeps away,
It runs softly back to the wilderness.
The moon is still alive,
But the wolf has gone to sleep.

Anna Reid (11)
North Coast Integrated College

Fear

Fear smells like rotten eggs,
It tastes like milk sitting on the window sill for three weeks.
It sounds like wolves howling in the dark,
It feels like your friend just slapped you on a cold winter's night,
It looks like your worst nightmare.

Lauren Millar (11)
North Coast Integrated College

My Cricketing Friend

Everyone knows the game I play
think it makes no sense,
my family and me, play it every day
everyone else laughs and thinks
what an idiot I am!

Cricket, I play because it's fun
no one knows if I'm good or bad,
I cry and cry, every night
still no one comes.
But then one day a boy says,
'Do you want to play a game of cricket?'
I burst with excitement.
'Hooray, hooray!' I said, dancing.

I couldn't care whether anyone laughs anymore.
I've always got my friend . . .
That's the only thing that matters to me.

Matthew George Caulfield (11)
North Coast Integrated College

The Three Little Pigs

There once were three little pigs,
One made a house out of twigs,
The second made his out of straw,
He cut it with a rusted saw.
The last made his from bricks,
Which only took him two ticks.

The pigs were in the wood
And the wolf pulled up his hood.
He knocked on the first door
And said, 'I'm here to do my chore!'

So the pig let him in
And he snarled with a grin,
'And I'm now going to eat!
I'll start with his feet.'
The little pig said, 'No!
You'll just have to *go!*'

He went to the house made of straw,
And he offered the pig his paw.
And the little pig said, 'Neigh!
Get out and get on your way.'
And out of the house he went.

He came to the house made of bricks,
And he said, 'This time there'll be no tricks!'
But then he found to his surprise
That the third little pig, he was wise.
The house was so thick
'Cause it was made out of brick.
The wolf was so stuck,
He had run out of luck!
So he growled, 'I might as well go back to my hut!'

Stacey Kirgan (11)
North Coast Integrated College

Follow The River

In the cities, in the streets
Where on earth are we meant to meet?
Our friend Mary-Kate
Who helped us to escape,
Told us to go to a place
All of us had a worried face.
Are we near or far from the river?
Hope we are, because I want to start to shiver.
Then Michael found a way across
The river deep, where there was frost.
Oh no! Now what?
'I've got a cut, how I hope that it does clot.
Oh well, come on -
Look, there's a fire apon
Let's go quick and get some more sticks.
Quick, for the fire, we're all tired.
Now we can have a rest and eat the best.'
I put the pot on the fire with boiling water.
Where did she learn that I wonder? Mummy taught her?
'Come here Michael, this is hot.'
'I'm not putting my leg in that pot!'
'No Michael, I've got some cloths,
I'll tear them up to help stop the clot.
I'll wrap them around your sore leg
Until the pain goes away.
Now Peggy, what do you want?'
'I found a rabbit when I went out to hunt.'
'We can't eat that, it might have been dead too long.'
Then Michael got a stone and it went *pong!*
Michael killed a rabbit, now we can eat.
I'll put it on the fire to heat.
Oh no! Now it's starting to rain -
Come on, let's follow the river again!

Nicole McElwee (11)
North Coast Integrated College

Honesty

Honesty is a rare thing now,
It eats away at your soul.
You have the urge to tell the truth,
Yet you hold back.

I believe my friends are honest with me,
But they always stab me in the back,
They tell me one thing and do the other.
Why do I even bother?

I too am dishonest,
I wish I could tell the truth!
Bare my soul to everyone.
Now I can see
The world's not for you, it's for me!

Michael McConnell (17)
North Coast Integrated College

Fantastic Food

Food is nice, food is great, food is brilliant,
Food is lovely to eat.
Food is beautiful, if you say it with rhyme.

There are different types of food.
Good food, bad food, small portions, large portions.
Save some room for dessert, because
The best part is dessert.

All the foods around the world are good.
Japanese food, Chinese food and also
Food from Turkey.

High quality foods
Medium quality foods
Low quality foods.

Now you know some things about food.
So I hope you will start eating different food.

Stuart Kane (11)
North Coast Integrated College

A Perfect Dream

A summer breeze, a shining sun,
On the beach with a special someone.
A silent whisper, a teasing hug,
A gentle kiss, a sense of love.
The glistening water, the clear blue sky.
All alone, just him and I,
Watching the waves glide to and fro.
Happy memories, no more woe.
The warm sand, the fresh air
A beautiful sight for us to share.
A journey filled with love and fear
A struggle only the heart will bear.
A fight within this heart of mine,
As if these feelings were a crime.
Exciting like a roller coaster,
Frightening like a thunderstorm.
Despite the feelings, just like this,
I still feel safe and warm -
On the roundabout of love.
My head is spinning round,
I know somehow that I won't fall,
When his arms are around.
Like a ball of fire, the sun finally begins to die.
We watch the darkness creeping in,
As it falls from the sky.
But in the distance, I hear a voice
Telling me to make a choice.
I wake up to an early morning call,
It was a perfect dream, that's all.

Christine Gogarty (13)
Rainey Endowed School

Peace

My tranquil wave of stillness
Swirls through the land like a motionless tornado.
Fiery flames will be quenched
As I pour over the craggy mountains
And glide down the fresh springs.
I am swimming in your mind, waiting
Waiting for an answer.
You can drink me now
Freely I dance,
Appearing temporarily,
Hitting your heart like
A powerful missile.
I will always remain near,
Ready for you
Willing you
To embrace me.
I burrow into hearts
Trying to embed myself.
Round and round the Earth
My spirit circles,
I want to stay forever,
Together for you.
I get dizzy -
Waiting for agreements,
Stop the fighting
Let me live.
Can I make a lasting appearance?

Gemma Donnelly (17)
Rainey Endowed School

The Big Day

'The big day has come,
But can he perform?'
The words spin around his head,
The manager is right
He will have to fight,
If he wants to win the cup.

He walks onto the pitch,
There's clapping and cheering.
He can hardly hear
But he knows what to do.
He has to,
He needs to score a goal.

The whistle blows and the match begins,
Playing with the breeze.
First shot missed, the second too,
Can he do what he has to do?

Second half and he's on a roll,
Nothing can stop him now,
Except maybe the man in goal.
What a shot!
What a save!
Oh so close to a goal!

Again he bursts forward
And he sees the goal,
But the defender sees it too.
He closes him down,
Slide tackle in the box,
Red card, penalty, goal and that's that.

Vincent McKenna (11)
St Mary's Grammar School, Magherafelt

My Family

My little sister Eimer,
Is seven years of age.
She is a little monkey,
Who should be locked up in a cage.

My older sister Niamh
She thinks I'm really tall
And she makes fun of me
Just because she's small

I call my father 'Da'
And he thinks it's really funny
But I know that he doesn't mind
'Cause I'm his little honey

My mum is very special
She does lot of things for me
She helps me with my homework
And never stops making tea

I have a cat called Felix
Who's the softest of our bunch
He sits upon your lap
When he knows it's time for lunch

There is one last person in this rhyme
And this is fabulous me!
I wrote a poem about the people
Who complete my family.

Katie McGuckian (13)
St Mary's Grammar School, Magherafelt

My Room

I have a room
A purple room
It can sometimes be
Called the 'Tunnel Of Doom'.

Because of the mess
I leave round my bed
'Tidy your room,'
My mum said.

I have a bed, a wardrobe
And a shelf
I try to keep my room tidy
All by myself.

So my room can be messy,
Nice or clean.
And I hope some day
It will be fit for a teen.

Johanna McAuley (12)
St Mary's Grammar School, Magherafelt

Autumn

Multicoloured tears floating from Heaven
A colourful patchwork quilt forming on the ground
Leaves are little pieces of a rainbow that have fallen off.

Thick, cloudy and grey is the fog, roaming free
It is an experimental gas bubbling and thick
It is hard to see in the fog, it gets you lost.

Dormant lie the animals who are hibernating
They are like an empty room motionless
They are unaware of what is going on around them.

Wings flapping let you know
That a hundred angel-like birds are flying away
Their noise lets the people know they are going.

The moon turns golden by the light of the sun
It is like a shiny coin on black paper
It is the light that melts the heart at night.

Michael Mullan (12)
St Mary's Grammar School, Magherafelt

Remember This
(For my brother Conár who I will always love and miss with all my heart)

When you think that you're alone and that no one understands -
Just remember my name and that I'm here to hold your hand.
Although you may feel down and that things aren't going right,
I'll be there to say I love you and I'm here to hold you tight.

The hugs, the kisses, the laughter, everything that was said,
Think of all the fun we had as you lay by yourself in bed.
Although you think the world will end and life's not worth the while,
Remember all the good times and that will make you smile.

Remember that I'm here with you and that I'm going to be,
An angel who watches over you and everything I will see.
When danger lies ahead, I will guide you through it all.
Don't you worry my dear friend, cos I'm not gone at all.

Damhnáit Mc Hugh (13)
Thornhill College

Depression

Look at them criticise
Hear them as they laugh,
Pointing at me as if I was a freak
With a neck like a mini giraffe.

Try to make small conversation
Talking, but nothing's said.
They say I have the biggest ego
But really, I wish I was dead.

The little ones look at me
As if I was a lion in a zoo.
Just stand there gazing, saying,
'I wish I was you.'

I only have trouble with the *adults*
But children still they are,
If they keep wasting their time on *boys*
Their future won't go far.

I wish I was someone else
Not a *star,* cos I don't care.
I only want to have a life
Where everyone starts being fair.

Deborah Boyle (14)
Thornhill College

Single Ticket

I'll get a cheaper ticket to misery next time
Don't you think a lifetime of isolation was enough?
For a first class seat, on the solitude bus.

An express train to seclusion
A quick flight to pain
I'd give them my heart, my spirit, my core
Why? They'd reject me all the same . . .

Éimear Barr (13)
Thornhill College

Our World

Look around at the world
and tell me what you see?
Racism, war
hurt and poverty.

Ask yourself, who are we -
and can we stop this mess?
As a world, we can do something
about it and forget the past.

So what if people are black?
Who cares if people are white?
We are all still people
and deserve to be treated right.

Look at the lives destroyed,
people living in fear.
What have we created?
if only God were here.

Let's join hands together
try to put things right.
It'll put an end to all the tears
and it'll be a good sight.

Stacey Concannon (13)
Thornhill College

Poetry In Motion

Arms moving,
Feet kicking,
Water splashing everywhere
As I glide through the water
As fast as I can.

On my tiptoes in the hall
Being as quiet as I can.
I am creeping about
Looking for a pot of jam!

Hannah Mahon (12)
Thornhill College

War

People in this world
Started a war
All because of oil!
Now the world has been spoiled,
It is completely destroyed,
Man's ability to create war
And hate, is not what God wants.
But man thinks only of his greed for wealth.
These people act like things are normal,
Whilst they attend a meeting which is formal,
They decide to start a feud
And to destroy lives,
To wreck families
To kill those who are dearly loved.
To kill young children,
Who can't defend themselves.
And why?
All because of their own greed.

Eimear Doherty (11)
Thornhill College

I Want To Be Free From Society

Why can't we just be free
And just be what we want to be?
Instead we do things just to please
The judgmental people in society

Some people are thin, some are fat
But so what - God made them like that!
People are afraid to be themselves
And put themselves up on the shelves.

They hide away not even daring
To come out in case of staring
Why can't people just break free
And be the person they want to be?

Nikita McChrystal (13)
Thornhill College

Gone!

Tick-tock
The clock stops
Because you've gone.

The world stands still
The glass half filled
Because you've gone.

Every day and night
My heart calls your name
I'm still afraid to turn off the light
Because I hate the fact
That I'm alone.

You were taken so young
Each day now a bitter taste
My life is such a waste
Because you're no longer at my side.

Come back, come back
I miss you so much
I really wish it wasn't your time to go

I loved you so much
But now you will never know.

Tick-tock
The clock stops
It's time to say my goodbyes
Dear Anna-Marie
You will always be missed
By me.

Rachael Page (13)
Thornhill College

I Just Want To Be Free

I want to tell them my opinion,
But will they really care?
I try to tell them something,
But it's like I'm not even there.

I want to show them everything,
Everything I can be.
I want them to know
I just want to be free.

As I sit here
People walk by.
I'm calling to them
But they don't hear me cry.

They look at me
Then walk on.
It's annoying when they do that
It's like I don't belong.

I want to get out of here,
No one cares for me.
Will somebody listen?
I just want to be free!

Anna McKinney (14)
Thornhill College

Dancing

Twisting this way and that
To keep up with the beat.
Hopping about on your feet,
Arms flinging in all directions,
To keep the dance to perfection.

Clódagh McBay (12)
Thornhill College

Poetry In Motion

The race has started, off I go
Jumping over obstacles,
Twisting, writhing, over that bar.
My legs go shaky as I sprint,
Trembling in case I lose.

Creeping under low nets,
Walking on a tightrope.
I'm swaying dangerously,
Dodging through poles.
I'm nearly there!

Shivering as I swim through cold water,
Running through the woods.
Climbing up a rope, I see the finish line,
I've won!
So I shall wave as I go!

Gemma Houston (11)
Thornhill College

September 11th

Should they laugh or should they cry?
Should they live or should they die?
Should they be the ones to suffer,
Under the country and its mother?
Would their families mourn and weep
And hang black banners in the street?
Should they stand up and say,
They're sorry for what they did that day.
Should they see the aftermath,
See the innocence that suffered their wrath?
Would they feel remorse and sorrow,
Wishing they could die tomorrow?
Would they look into their hearts and find
A bit of them, they left behind?

Róisín Lautman (13)
Thornhill College

Poetry In Motion

I'm at the circus
I can see dancers in front of me
Twisting about, shaking their bodies.
There're people in the background
Skipping, jumping and hopping about.

The crowds are swaying.
The children are shouting,
The funny clown is waving
Hello to everyone.

Now it's time to go home.
We're driving home and the
Children are crying -
I'm falling asleep. Zzzzzz.

Laura Doherty (11)
Thornhill College

The Farm

My friends say the farm stands motionless
But I could see, feel and hear everything
I could see the windvane twisting to the north
I could hear the wind gliding through the air towards me.
As I drew nearer to the barn
I could feel my skin twitching and my bones shaking,
But I knew in my heart I was not afraid.
I could feel the leaves dance around me.
I caught a glimpse of spiders creeping up
The rotted barn and heard the carthorse gallop behind me
I turned in a flash and ran - and until this day I have
Carried that memory deep down inside.

Lauren McDaid (13)
Thornhill College

Poetry In Motion

Looking out of my bedroom window,
I saw him running down the lane,
Shivering frantically, in amongst the falling rain.

Suddenly a bolt of lightning struck him from the back like that,
Swaying on the single spot.
Fell in the mud with a *splat!*

Putting on my dressing gown, listening for a sound.
The clock was ticking down the stairs.
The toys were on the ground.

I sneak the back door open and creep out into the yard,
Trudging through the mud and rain, starting to go hard.

I see the old man lying there, I shiver to see his face.
Scabbed and bruised and cut all over
With his hand on top of a suitcase.

But then the old man's eyes opened up,
But where the eyes should be, there was
Nothing but empty sockets!

I screamed a kind of muffled scream
And sprinted up the lane.
Ran up the stairs and into my room -
Never to go down again!

Claire Cassidy (12)
Thornhill College

Autumn

Kicking, prancing and jumping on the red, yellow, orange and brown,
Putting my scarf on to go and play with them in my busy little town.
Patiently waiting for the other children to come along and join,
Waving the crisp leaves floating through the air,
Flying in the sky, like a free bird without a care.

Natasha Deeney (13)
Thornhill College

Poetry In Motion

I am a very active girl.
I like to jump and run and swirl.
I move a lot all through the day
And that I am very proud to say!

I just have to dance and twist a lot.
I like the feeling of being hot.
I like to creep and hop around
And keep on doing it 'til I drop to the ground.

At night-time when it's time to calm down
I get very sad and put on a frown,
But in my sleep I twitch around
And I then wake up when I fall to the ground.

Sophie Dechant (13)
Thornhill College

Poetry In Motion

She keeps time with the music
Her feet barely touch the ground,
Jumping to the heavens
Landing without a sound

She's gently dancing upon the floor
Twisting as she goes,
She jumps high in the air
Crossing her little toes.

She swirls
She leaps
As lightly as she goes
Dancing with all her *trusting*
Trusted might
She's surely an angel in delight.

Rebecca Harkin
Thornhill College

Moving

There are a lot of things that I like to do
That involve lots of moving.
I especially like skipping and
sometimes jumping.

I like walking, but I like running better,
I also like to dance, but also writing a letter.

When I'm cold I'm always trembling.
Mostly I'm cold when I'm in Assembly.

Hopping, swimming, I like a lot,
But shaking and shivering I do not!

When I see my friends I'm always waving.
I like it when a lifeguard's saving.

Sprinting, twisting, swaying.
I'm always on the move.
Twitching and creeping puts me in
a bad mood.

Gliding through the air on an aeroplane in the sky.
Up there I wish I could fly.

Milissa Deane (13)
Thornhill College

Poetry In Motion

I was out there, dancing
Under the disco ball.
Showing off my best moves
Everyone was watching me,
Everyone was shouting, 'Jonny! Jonny!'
I then did the splits.
The lights were flashing all around me.
Then all you could hear was the creak
And I ended up in hospital!

Áine Laughlin (11)
Thornhill College

Love

Love has so many meanings,
It could have a happy or a sad ending.
Your emotions can change in many different ways,
You may feel like you love someone but they don't even love you.

Love has so many meanings,
What could a girl want more?
This emotion might fade away
Then you love someone more.

Love, does it have so many meanings?
Maybe, maybe not!
It may bring happiness, marriage, sadness or break-up,
Or it may bring something more!

Love has many reasons, lots of different things,
First of all comes family love,
Second comes teenage love.
Finally, love may come for life.
But . . . to me love means everything!
Dearbhla McEleney (11)
Thornhill College

Dancing

'Dance!' said the woman to the man.
Away he went, to dance the best he can.
Nice and easy, singing and swaying,
Creeping around gently on the ground.
Inside the castle they danced all day,
Night-time came and they had to go away.
'Goodnight!' said the man.
'Goodnight!' said the woman.
'We shall dance again!'
Cara Duddy (12)
Thornhill College

The Tide

Crash! The wave breaks and the white water hisses
and slithers like angry snakes struggling onto land,
but the sea stretches out an invisible arm and
pulls it back to claim it into its vast belly.

Crash! The wave breaks and water surges forward.
Try harder! Try harder! Before the arm pulls it back
to the dark cold depths and it gives up.

Crash! The wave breaks and the water slithers and
twists and struggles before the arm pulls it back
and on goes the tide.
Push and pull, push and pull!

Una Kelly (12)
Thornhill College

Poetry In Motion

I'm in the pool, swimming with my friends.
We're jumping and splashing and having fun.
I stand on the edge and jump right in.
I go down the slide and feel the cool water
Splash my skin.

After swimming, we go for a run.
My leg got sore so I didn't have fun.
I fell to the ground and howled with pain,
And to make it even worse, it started to rain!

I got up quickly and hopped away
And I stayed inside for the rest of the day!

Seanna Meehan (11)
Thornhill College

War

As they march, getting closer and closer
singing and chanting all the way
As they come face to face
standing still with fear in their eyes

At the sound of a horn, they start to charge
First the foot soldiers, followed by
the soldiers on horses
Canons fire, guns shoot -
as one by one they fall.

After a long and bloody fight
only few have survived
They take a look around
and see if they can find any familiar faces

When they are all sent home
they are happy and sad
For they are grateful that they survived
but sad for those who died.

Aoife McTernan (12)
Thornhill College

Poetry In Motion

When I am at the park
I can see the leaves shivering on the trees
and the rabbits hopping on the grass.
I see the birds flying and the fish swimming.
I see the children skipping and the dogs running,
I can see the swing swaying
and the boats gliding on the water.
I can see the rain cloud creeping in
and I can't wait to go home.

Clare McLaughlin (13)
Thornhill College

Where Is The Love?

One cold and frosty night
Two countries began to fight.
What a terrible idea this was
Simply because . . .

People are killed,
Children hurt, listen to them crying.
Look at this sadness
Please take away the badness!

The war is over now
I can feel the sunshine.
I can see Heaven
Somewhere amongst the clouds.

Sarah Wallace (12)
Thornhill College

Poetry In Motion

Running, skipping, jumping
They're the things I like to do
Dancing, swaying, twisting
They're the things me and you do

Twisting in the morning
Twitching at night
Shivering outside, that would give you a fright.

Gliding on the ice rink
Dancing outside
Jumping outside to see if I can
Touch the sky, so high.

Martina Murray (13)
Thornhill College

The Wind

As I stepped outside the door
I heard the strong wind roar,
The wind blew past all the trees
Knocking down all the leaves.

The sky was gloomy and dark
As the lightning struck with a great big spark.
I tried to run down the street
But the wind blew strong and lifted me off my feet.

Back to the house I ran, in a hurry
The wind, it howled with a raging fury.
The dogs outside yelped and struggled
But in my bed I was warm and snuggled.

Eimear McIvor (11)
Thornhill College

My Birthday

My birthday is in May,
I can't wait until that brilliant day.
I'll have lots of food, balloons and toys
And definitely *no boys!*
I'll have music and games
And a trampoline.
Oh, I'm so keen!
Until that day comes, I'll sit and wait
And never forget that wonderful date.
My birthday will be a big surprise,
I can't wait to see it with my own eyes.

Sharon Duffy (11)
Thornhill College

S Club 8

I love S Club 8
I think they are great.

Hannah is always dancing
Whilst Frankie is busy romancing.

Daisy is always playing with her hair
And Rochelle is telling the boys to play fair.

Aaron is the oldest member of the band
Jay is always ready to give a helping hand.

Stacey loves sweets
And sometimes she has them for treats.

Calvin is the sort of bloke
That when you see him you would choke.

Calvin will always be in my heart
And if I meet him we will never part!

Orla Hegarty (11)
Thornhill College